The Key of David

Living as a
Priest, a Prophet and a King!

Discovering what it means to live in the fullness that
God has intended His sons and daughters to be in.

Günther A. Schenk

Copyright © 2010 by Günther A Schenk, All rights reserved.

ISBN Number: 978-99945-71-02-4

Editor: Ester du Toit
Cover and Graphic Design: Haiko Bruns
Printing: John Meinert Printing (PTY) LTD.

First edition 2010

© All rights reserved. No part of this book may be reproduced, stored in a retrieval system, or transmitted in any form or by any means, electronic, photocopying, recording or by any other means available, without prior written permission from the author.

Unless otherwise indicated, all scripture quotations are taken from the NEW AMERICAN STANDARD BIBLE ®, Copyright © 1960, 1962, 1963, 1968, 1971, 1972, 1973, 1975, 1977, 1995 by The Lockman Foundation. Used by permission.

Definitions are taken from Strong's Concordance, Thayer's Greek Definitions and Webster's Dictionary as indicated.

For more information contact:
Lion of Judah Ministries
PO Box 80236, Windhoek, Namibia
E-mail: office @ lionofjudahmin.com
Web: www.lionofjudahmin.com

DEDICATION

I dedicate this book to my loving wife, Beatrix, who has been a support and an inspiration to me in so many ways. You are a precious gift of God, and I cannot think how I would live without you! You bring so much joy and perspective in many things. You truly are a 'help meet' from God.

May the Lord move you from strength to strength.

I love you dearly.

CONTENTS

Acknowledgements 6
Foreword 7
Introduction 8

Chapter One – Keys of the Spirit 11
    Keys in the singular form
    Keys in the plural form
Application Study Guide for Chapter One 30

Chapter Two – Restoring the Tabernacle of David 31
Application Study Guide for Chapter Two 35

Chapter Three – The Key of David: Position and Dimensions 39
    What position?
    What dimension/s?
    Bringing the two together
    Summary
Application Study Guide for Chapter Three 46

Chapter Four – The Dimension of the Priest 47
Application Study Guide for Chapter Four 53

Chapter Five – The Dimension of the Prophet 55
Application Study Guide for Chapter Five 60

Chapter Six – The Dimension of the King 61
Application Study Guide for Chapter Six 67

Chapter Seven – Understanding and functioning in the Times of God 69
    Unlocking the kairos time of God
    Teach me to number my days
    Discerning the times of God and what to do in them
    Definitions used in Chapter Seven
Application Study Guide for Chapter Seven 91

Chapter Eight – Moving into the Order of Melchizedek 93
Application Study Guide for Chapter Eight 96

Chapter Nine – In Conclusion 97

Bibliography 99

ACKNOWLEDGEMENTS

All the glory is due to the Lord Jesus Christ who gives revelation and insight of His Word through His Holy Spirit. Thank you Lord for leading and guiding me step by step! All praise, honour and glory are due to You!

No meaningful work can ever be attributed to one person, and therefore I give acknowledgement to the following people who have laid foundations in my life concerning the apostolic ministry.

To Dr. Jonathan and Helen David, whom the Lord has used in a powerful way to transform my life and that of my dearest wife, Beatrix. Thank you for being an instrument in the Lord's hand and an inspiration to do the Father's will.

I want to specially thank Cas and Laetitia Becker for their constant love and support, which they have given my wife and myself, as well as this ministry that the Lord has entrusted to us. Their encouragement in times of difficulty has made it possible to stay focused on the Lord and His calling for us. You have been a blessing and support in many ways.

No person can stand without friends and I thank the Lord for allowing me to know so many precious people. It is not possible to mention every person, so to all those who have been praying for us, especially the intercessors of Lion of Judah Ministries, and those sowing financially into this ministry and also towards this project, we thank you for your sacrifice and for allowing the Lord to use you as instruments in His hands. We appreciate you greatly.

A big thank you to Ernst Kubirske, who has believed in us, encouraged us and committed himself to stand and serve with us in this calling, you are truly a blessing.

Lastly I would like to thank Ester for all her work in editing this book, and her husband, Manie, together with Wilhelm and Joleen for very specifically praying for this project and carrying it close to your heart from the beginning stages.

Reference in this work has been made to books and teachings composed by Dr. Jonathan David, Apostle Thamo Naidoo and Rev. Michael Pitts (listed alphabetically) and use of such reference is indicated. I have made use of the main concept given by the mentioned person and have then expanded on these main points. I give honour to these men and the work they have done in the Kingdom of God.

FOREWORD

In today's world the church has a vital role to fulfil. In order to do that it has to understand the keys in God's word. There are so many other powers that aspire to be "the solution" to mankind's problems, and yet nothing is improving. Whether you believe in an end-time scenario or not, the truth is that the world is in a bad shape and probably the worst is still to come. As this reality is speaking to the church, the church needs to rise up and become the answer for the world again.

We are admonished in Heb 5 and 6 to go on to maturity. We, the church as a body, and also as individuals, need to realise that maturity to walk in the revelation of Jesus Christ and His power is a must. 'Playing Christians' will not be a solution to mankind's problems; only those with a laser focus who use the keys of authority given to them in the Word of God will be a solution.

In this book Günther set out the necessary keys we need to make a difference in this world. The word of God is not complicated, and when we receive the necessary revelation, faith will rise, maturity will come, and confidence will be the order of the day. This book is for those who are serious in their walk with God; this is not milk but solid food for those who hunger after a deeper reality in the presence of God. Günther made a careful study out of which flowed this excellent book.

You need to live in the revelation of being "in Christ". You need to know how to discern God's Kairos moments for your life and take full advantage of them. If you are hungry, study this book; meditate on it until you have the full revelation of your position as king, priest and prophet and the dimensions that go with that.

May you become the man and woman of authority God called you to be. May you not be one of those who are missing the mark through compromise and the lack of hunger to be the best. May they say of you that what they said of Jesus:
"…..the people were amazed at the things he said, because he spoke with authority" (Luke 4:32 NLT).

Cas Becker
Senior Pastor, Agapé Windhoek Congregation

INTRODUCTION

"And to the angel of the church of Philadelphia write: He who is holy, who is true, who has the key of David, who opens and no one will shut, and who shuts and no one opens, says this:"

Rev 3:7

Much has been spoken and written about the 'Key of David' mentioned in this verse, but we also need to understand that the Lord not only brings revelation to His people but He also brings progressive revelation. It is a building process that the Lord does in our lives, one level upon another, and one precept upon another.

I believe the revelations brought to you in this book will take you to the next level in your walk with God, and are of utmost importance if the Body of Christ is to function in the fullness that the Lord Jesus Christ has called us to function in. God desires you to draw closer in relationship with Him, and the outflow of that will be that you will become more effective in doing His Kingdom work.

Whether you are an individual, a congregation or a ministry, these principles and truths that follow will enable you to be more effective, not just in His Kingdom, but they will propel your personal relationship with the Lord into new dimensions, allowing you to move accurately in the destiny that He has for you!

I have been challenged by the Lord to include a study guide after each chapter to help you work through the revelations given so that the Holy Spirit can solidify the truths in your heart. This will cause you not to just have the revelation, but to actually live it.

A few years ago the Lord gave me a vision of a shaft of light coming down out of heaven. All around the light there was darkness. I saw many people who were walking around the light.

The Lord spoke clearly to me saying that all those walking around the light are seeing the light but they are still in darkness because they are not in the light. So it is with Christians who can see the light but are actually still living in darkness. Revelation works in much the same way. We ask God to give us revelation, and we receive it, but we fail to walk in that revelation! It is because of this truth that many children of God fail to break through in their lives – there is a great difference between *having* a revelation and *living* in that revelation.

After speaking this, the Lord then gave me the same picture with one difference: there was a person inside the shaft of light ministering to the people from within the light. Many miracles took place and prayers were answered and although the person inside the light could not clearly see into the darkness, he was led by the Spirit of God in what to do with incredible accuracy.

When we start functioning from within the light and life of God we will see dramatic changes taking place in and through our lives! If you live the revelation (living in the revelation), then you will see things change that have never been moved before!

Please do not rush through the book just to say that 'I have read it'. I challenge you to allow the Holy Spirit to guide and instruct you as you read each chapter and as you work through the study guide provided. Let all that is written become principles that you live by in your walk with our Lord.

Tips on how to approach the 'Application Study Guide' at the end of each chapter.

- Pray and ask the Lord to take you deeper and to challenge you further as you answer the questions.
- The questions are there to serve as guidelines to help you to become more focussed with the topic at hand. You will find that the Lord will start guiding and leading you step-by-step, even just in the reading of each chapter.
- Do not be 'mechanical' in answering the questions, but rather let the Holy Spirit stir you and prompt you.
- Allow God to show you where you are now in your relationship with Him, and where He wants to take you to. It is important that you allow God to bring alignment into your life; in order for this to happen, you must know where you are and where you are headed.
- Take time for each question and do not rush the work of the Spirit in your life.

Declare this today:

"Lord I am willing to allow you to work in my life so that I may be a vessel of honour for your purposes. I want to live the dream that You have for my life. Lord give me revelation and help me to function in that revelation! Amen."

CHAPTER ONE

KEYS OF THE SPIRIT

Keys speak of authority because they have the ability to lock and unlock doors. From the Strong's concordance 'key' is understood to be a key (as in *shutting* a lock), literally or figuratively: (G2807. kleis; *klice*).

Therefore, if you have a key, you can enter in and go out, as well as being able to prevent other people from coming in or going out. Understanding that keys can be used in the spiritual sense too, as seen in our definition, we need to realise that God has given us very specific keys that are at our disposal. Unfortunately we cannot use the keys if we do not know the following:
- Do you have a key in your hand? It is not about how big the door is that needs to be opened (or shut); it depends on whether or not you have the key (authority) to open the door.
- Secondly: How well does the key fit that you are holding? Do you actually have the right key (authority) in your hand or not? You may have authority, but it may not be the authority for that door.
- The final factor in this is whether you are in actual fact standing before the right door! You may have the right authority but you may be standing in front of the wrong door.

The Bible teaches us that there are keys in the singular form and keys in the plural form. Allow me to explain some of these keys to you in more detail.

KEYS IN THE SINGULAR FORM:

1. The Key of the Abyss (bottomless pit): This is mentioned in Rev 9:1 and Rev 20:1. This is the key that opens and closes the bottomless pit and is held by an angel. Jesus can use it too, as we see in the legion of demons imploring Jesus not to send them to the abyss in Luke 8:30&31.
2. The key of David: Rev 3:7&8 shows us that this is a key that opens and shuts doors in the spirit. This key belongs to Jesus but he can confer it on those He chooses (Isa 22:22). We will explore this key in more detail later on, as I firstly need to lay foundations for some of the other keys, because there is a connection between some of them and this one.
3. The key of Knowledge: "Woe to you lawyers! For you have taken away the key of knowledge[1]; you yourselves did not enter, and you hindered those who were entering." Luke 11:52

1　　Strong's concordance: Knowledge – G1108 from G1097. gnōsis; *gno'-sis* Knowing (the act), that is, (by implication) *knowledge*: - knowledge, science.

The word knowledge here means by implication knowledge or science, and is taken from a root word[2] that means 'to know' in a great variety of applications. This key opens the way to revelation knowledge so that one can enter into the fullness of the Kingdom of Heaven and it is to be used by all. In Matt 23:13 Jesus very directly rebukes the Pharisees because they are hindering the people from entering into the Kingdom of Heaven.

In Luke 11:52 the word 'lawyers' is directly connected to the scripture in Matt 23:13. How do the Pharisees, a representation of the religious system, hinder people from entering into the Kingdom of Heaven? Simply by withholding the knowledge they require to gain access! The key of knowledge is used mainly by those in spiritual leadership, but is meant for every child of God!

There is a very interesting scripture in Proverbs that helps us to 'unlock' a part of this mystery. It says: "The Lord by wisdom[3] founded the earth, by understanding[4] He established the heavens. By His knowledge[5] the deeps were broken up and the skies drip with dew." Prov 3:19&20

It is clear to see that wisdom, understanding and knowledge are three different things. God formed the earth through His wisdom but by His understanding (which speaks of a different dimension) He formed the heavens. However, it was His knowledge that broke open the depths of all He had created and it is by this knowledge that we gain revelation to enter into the fullness of the Kingdom of Heaven. The root word, as given by Strong's concordance (H3045), used for knowledge, literally means '(cause to, let or make) know, (come to give, have, take) knowledge, (be, make, make to be, make self) known, be learned. It is when the depths of God's Kingdom are broken open, that 'the skies will drip with dew', meaning that the anointing of the Holy Spirit is released to us so that we may function in the Kingdom.

Rom 11:33 says that the depth of the riches of His wisdom and knowledge are too deep to be understood and that His ways are unsearchable[6]. However, in Jam 1:5 it says: "But if any of you lacks wisdom[7], let him ask God, who gives to all generously and without reproach, and it will be given to him."

---

2   Knowledge – G1097. ginōskō, ghin-oce'-ko: A prolonged form of a primary verb; to "know" (absolutely), in a great variety of applications and with many implications (as shown at left, with others not thus clearly expressed):
allow, be aware (of), feel, (have) known (-ledge), perceive, be resolved, can speak, be sure, understand.).

3   Strong's concordance: Wisdom – H2451, chokmâh, khok-maw'; From H2449; wisdom (in a good sense): -skillful, wisdom, wisely, wit.

4   Understanding – H8394, taw-boon', teb-oo-naw', to-boo-naw', The second and third forms being feminine; from H995; intelligence; by implication an argument; by extension caprice: -discretion, reason, skilfulness, understanding, wisdom.

5   Knowledge – H1847, dah'-ath, From H3045; knowledge: -cunning, [ig-] norantly, know(-ledge), [un-] awares (wittingly).

6   Unsearchable – G419, anexereunētos, an-ex-er-yoo'-nay-tos, From G1 (as a negative particle) and a presumed derivative of G1830; not searched out, that is, (by implication) inscrutable: - unsearchable.

7   Wisdom – G4678, sophia, sof-ee'-ah, From G4680; wisdom (higher or lower, worldly or spiritual): - wisdom.

So although scripture says that God's ways are unsearchable or hidden from us, it also says that He will 'cause us to know' or 'will come to give knowledge' if we ask Him for wisdom and understanding, so that we can move into the fullness with Him because this is His desire for us. To unlock the wisdom and understanding of God is using the key of knowledge because the knowledge of God is what opens the depths!

Jam 3:13-18 goes further in saying that you can draw from one of two sources of wisdom: If you have selfish ambition and bitter jealousy in your life, it will lead to wisdom that is "...earthly, natural, demonic" and is not from the Lord. Yet the wisdom that is from the Lord will lead you to have the fruit of righteousness. It is interesting to note that Satan, right from the beginning, wanted to cause mankind to draw from the wrong source. One source is from *the* tree of Life, that is Christ, and the other is from *the* tree of the knowledge of good and evil, that represents Satan (Gen 2:9). The enemy used the tree of the knowledge of good and evil as a shortcut to knowledge so that Adam and Eve would not depend on God, but rather on him.

We read in Gen 3:1-5 that Satan said to Eve that she would be like God, knowing good and evil, if she ate from the fruit of the tree of the knowledge of good and evil. It was at this point that the 'source change' of knowledge came. The lie that needs to be exposed here is the very fact that we are created in God's image and likeness (Gen 1:26&27) and that He will supply to us all knowledge as we ask of Him (Jam 1:5).

Another deception that the enemy has brought into our lives is for us to question why God placed the tree of the knowledge of good and evil in the garden. Many people have the perspective that God tempts us, and that it is for this reason that He placed the tree in the garden. The Word, though, is very clear in saying that God does not tempt us in any way (Jam 1:13&14) but that it is He who delivers the righteous out of temptation (2 Pet 2:9; 1 Cor 10:13).

The tree of the knowledge of good and evil was placed in the garden simply so that we can exercise our will. Man was called to have dominion over the earth (Gen 1:26), but how could he have dominion over the earth if he never learned to take charge of his own will! Man was to exercise his will so that he could learn to have dominion over the earth in the fullness God intended him to have.

So the enemy will do everything in his power to hinder you from using the key of Knowledge, because as you use this key, the Holy Spirit will start to reveal the depths of God to you and the enemy definitely does not want you to have this depth of revelation! Not only will you have the revelation, but also you will be able to function in the Kingdom of Heaven.

KEYS IN THE PLURAL FORM:

1. *The keys of Death and Hades:* Rev 1:18. Let it suffice to say that these are keys that give authority to judge for eternity, and Jesus holds them. He took

them back from the enemy when He went to the depths of hell, and rose victorious when the Glory of the Father came upon Him (Rom 6:4).
2. *The keys of the Kingdom of Heaven:* These keys are used to bind and loose things on the earth as they are in heaven (Matt 16:19; Matt 18:18). To fully comprehend how to use these keys, we need to look at four different aspects:

A. Revelation of nine principles of the Kingdom of Heaven

> "Pray, then, in this way:
> 'Our Father who is in heaven,
> Hallowed be Your name.'"
>
> Matt 6:9

When Jesus said, "Pray, then, in this way" He was not telling us to merely just repeat the words of His prayer, but to pray according to the principles that He revealed through this specific prayer.

I. Principle #1 – "Our Father": You firstly need to realise that you have a Father with Whom you have a relationship that needs to be continuously built. He is a loving Father Who desires just the best for you and me, and He has a destiny planned for each one of us. Scripture clearly tells us that we are sons of the living God, if led by the Holy Spirit, and that we have received the Spirit of Adoption (Rom 8:14&15). It is for this reason that we can say 'our' or 'my' Father.

II. Principle #2 – "…who is in heaven": God the Father dwells in heaven, but it is His desire is to be with us. It is for this reason that the Holy Spirit came after Christ's ascension so that the Father can be with us, and we can be in the Father's presence on earth until, one day, we will be with Him. To understand the term 'heaven' we need to look at its Hebrew and Greek meanings. In actual fact, there are three heavens and they are as follows:

The First Heaven: or otherwise known as the 'Atmospheric heaven', is a physical realm (touch, sight and smell) where the earth, the sun and moon, other stars and the solar systems are placed. The Hebrew word Shâmayim, shâmeh (shaw-mah'-yim, shaw-meh') refers to this heaven, and is defined in the Strong's concordance as follows: H8064; (The second form being dual of an unused singular); from an unused root meaning *to be lofty*; the *sky* (as aloft; the dual perhaps alluding to the visible arch in which the clouds move, as well as to the higher ether where the celestial bodies revolve): - air, X astrologer, heaven (-s). Reference to this is made in Gen 1:8; Gen 2:1; 2 Chron 6:18; Neh 9:6. For a quick geography lesson on the atmospheric heaven, using earth as our point of reference, we can see that there are four layers namely:

a) The Troposphere is the life-sustaining layer of air around the earth we live on and contains 90% of the air in the atmosphere. Its distance is from 0 to 15km above mean sea level.

b) The Stratosphere is where the ozone layer is found that absorbs the ultra violet rays from the sun. Long distance aircraft fly in the lower part and take advantage of the low air density. It ranges from approximately 15km to 50km above mean sea level.

c) The Ionosphere starts at 50km above mean sea level and ends at approximately 400 km above mean sea level. Particles called ions are in this layer and radio signals are 'bounced off' this layer. Satellites and other communication devices orbit the earth in this layer and as meteorites enter it they burn up.

d) The Exosphere has its start at approximately 400km above mean sea level, and 'containing' only a few particles of hydrogen and helium, we also call this 'layer' space where our galaxy and all other solar systems are found.

- Keep in mind that angelic and demonic beings can manifest themselves in the first heaven.

The Second Heaven: referred to as 'Heavenly places' in scripture (Eph 1:3,10,20&21; Eph 2:6; Eph 6:12; Rev 12:9&10) is a literal but spiritual place. The word 'literal' does not mean physical, but simply that it exists. According to the Strong's concordance the word heavenly, mentioned in the scriptures above, means the following: Epouranios, ep-oo-ran'-ee-os, From G1909 and G3772; *above* the *sky:* - celestial, (in) heaven (-ly), high.

a) It is a spirit place that exists although we cannot see it. When Scripture speaks about being 'in the spirit', it is talking about a spiritual position and ability that we have because of Christ (Rom 8:9).

b) In Eph 2:6 it says that we are seated with Christ in heavenly places. This refers to the second heaven and not, as we assume, to the throne room of God, or the Third Heaven.

c) Satan and his fallen angels operate from out of this spirit dimension (Eph 6:12). Some translations replace 'heavenly places' with 'high places' in this scripture, but the Greek meaning remains the same.

d) The word says that Christ is far above all rule and authority (Eph 1:20&21). Therefore, if we are seated with Christ in heavenly places, we are also far above all rule and authority of Satan. (I will elaborate more on this later.)

The Third Heaven: Strong's concordance defines this 'heaven' as: ouranos, *oo-ran-os'* G3772, Perhaps from the same as G3735 (through the idea of *elevation*); the sky; by extension *heaven* (as the abode of God); by implication *happiness, power, eternity;* specifically the *Gospel (Christianity):* - air, heaven ([-ly]), sky. Once again it is a literal but spiritual place and refers to the literal throne room of God. Scripture reference for the third heaven can be found in Matt 6:9&10; 2 Cor 12:2-4; Rev 4:1&2. Whatever God established in heaven He has given us a representation of on the earth. Looking at the Tabernacle of Moses, we see that there is an inner court, the Holy Place and the Holy of Holies. Although there are no definite rooms in heaven like in the tabernacle, there are three different 'areas', namely the Paradise of God, the Paradise of angels and the Paradise of man.

a) <u>The Paradise of God</u>[8] is represented by the Holy of Holies in the Tabernacle of Moses. This is where the literal person of the Father, Son and Holy Spirit dwell; it is the throne room of God. No angel or person goes into the paradise of God without being 'summoned' to the King! The only heavenly beings in the throne room are the winged creatures, the cherubim and seraphim.

- The word *cherubim* in Hebrew means 'those grasped or held fast'. A description of the cherubim is found in Eze 1:5-14. Here follows what we know about these heavenly beings:
  o They appear to be the highest rank of the created heavenly beings. Please remember that they are not angels! At this point I would like to mention that God did not create Satan! Satan was first known as 'the anointed cherub who covers' or, in some translations, as 'the guardian cherub' before his fall (Eze 28:14). This placed him in a higher rank than the cherubim and seraphim.
  o God sits enthroned between the cherubim (Ps 80:1; Ps 99:1) just as depicted on the mercy seat of the Ark of the Covenant (Ex 25:17-21).
  o They are powerful and are always associated with God's glory and moral perfection (Eze 1:15-28; Eze 9:3; Eze 10:1-22).
  o They serve as guardians of the Garden of Eden (Gen 3:24), and the most Holy place (Ex 25:18-22; Ex 26:31-33).
  o They follow the Spirit of God wherever it goes (Eze 1:12&20).

- The next heavenly beings we find in God's direct presence are the *seraphim*. The Hebrew word for seraphim means burning or noble. This is what we know about the seraphim:
  o They are always associated with, and show, God's holiness (Isa 6:2-4; Rev 4:6-8).

b) <u>The Paradise of Angels</u>[9] is associated with the Holy Place in the Tabernacle of Moses. As said, not every angel can come before the Shekinah Glory of God. The word *angel* means messenger or agent in the Hebrew, as is clear in Heb 1:14.

- Please note that the angels are not ours to command! They are God's angels and only His to command to do HIS bidding. We cannot pray to angels and tell them what to do. We make our request known to God, and He will command His angels as He sees fit.
- *Archangels* are the highest in rank among the angels. Michael is referred to as a 'prince' as mentioned in Dan 10:13&21 and Dan 12:1. Also see Jude 9. Gabriel is the only other archangel mentioned in scripture, and when he speaks, he brings understanding from God. Read Dan 8:15-17 and Dan 9:21&22 as well as Luke 1:19.
- What is the role of angels? Primarily angels are there to worship God (Heb 1:6&7. Also see Rev 5:11&12 and Rev 7:11&12). Other roles are to:
  o Fight against evil forces – Dan 10:13; 2 Kings 6:16:18; Rev

---

8   Reference is made to the DVD series "Pulling Down Strongholds" by Dr. Jonathan David.

9   Reference is made to the DVD series "Pulling Down Strongholds" by Dr. Jonathan David.

12:7/20:1&2. They are like a mighty army: 2 Sam 5:22-25; 2 Kings 6:17; Ps 34:7; Zech 1:8-10 (Zech 6:1-7).
- o Protect God's people – Ps 91:11&12; Dan 6:22; Gen 19:12.
- o Administer punishment/judgment – Gen 19:13; 2 Sam 24:16&17.
- o Relay messages from God to us – Matt 1:20.
- o Bring encouragement – Dan 10:12&18.
- o Bring guidance. Ministering angels direct the path of man – Ex 14:19.
- o Bring provision – Matt 4:11.

c) The inner court of the Tabernacle of Moses represents the <u>Paradise of man</u>[10], now known as the Father's house (John 14:2&3). When the righteous people die they go to the paradise of man, which is in the third heaven (or just 'heaven' as we know it). When God created heaven there was only a paradise of God and of angels. There was no need for a paradise of man, because through Jesus every saint in the Old Testament was saved. The only people who were in heaven before the resurrection of Christ were Enoch, Elijah and Moses, because God took them 'up' to Himself. All other saints were in paradise (Abraham's bosom; Luke 16:19-27) but were held captive and prevented from being in the Father's presence by Satan (Satan would not let his captives go home: Ps 102:19&20 and Isa 14:12-17 with the focus on verse 17).

After Jesus' resurrection, He went to the Father and cleansed the third heaven and recreated the paradise of man in heaven. There is more detail to this aspect, but let this suffice for now.

Within the paradise of man, there are different levels of 'glory'. This is according to the seed that was given to you and the maturity you brought to that seed while living on earth. God has created us with a purpose and destiny and we are to fulfil that purpose and it is according to this fulfilment of purpose that we will receive our 'crown of glory' (1 Cor 9:25; 1 Tim 4:7&8).

2 Tim 1:9 says "who has saved us and called us with a holy calling, not according to our works, but **according to His own purpose** and grace which was granted us in Christ Jesus from all eternity." (Bold print added).

In 1 Cor 15:20-58 Paul speaks of the resurrection of the dead and how the perishable becomes the imperishable, and how a natural body is raised as a spiritual body, etc. In the middle of the text is a verse that stands out to us: "There is one glory of the sun, and another of the moon, and another glory of the stars; **for star differs from star in glory.**" 1 Cor 15:41 (Bold print added)

---

[10] Reference is made to the DVD series "Pulling Down Strongholds" by Dr. Jonathan David.

The Bible says in numerous places that we will be judged according to our works/deeds and receive our reward accordingly (Ps 62:12; Prov 24:12; Rom 2:5-8; 1 Cor 3:11-13). Please note that this is after our salvation, which cannot be bought through works, but is built on our relationship with Christ alone! The 'work' speaks of whether we were obedient to what He gave us to do according to His purpose for us, and according to the measure in which we fulfilled it. Throughout the paradise of God, the paradise of angels and the paradise of man, the fullness of the presence of God is experienced because there are no partitions, or boundaries, between the different 'sections' or areas.

Remember the veil of the temple was torn in two, not just allowing us entrance to the Lord's throne room, but also allowing the fullness of Him to pass through to us! It is like sitting in a theatre watching a show. The people sitting in the back row see and experience exactly the same as the people sitting in the front row. You are just seated in a different position. Therefore, whether you are in the throne room of God or in the paradise of angels, or paradise of man, the intensity of His glory and presence remain the same throughout because it fills the third heaven!

In Rev 4 and 5 we clearly see this depicted. All is centred round the throne of God and moves outward in concentric circles. It is first God's throne, then the seven lamp stands and the seven spirits of God, then the cherubim and seraphim, then the twenty four thrones and the elders, and then the thousands of angels, all around His throne. What we read in these two chapters is prophetically depicted through the tabernacle (tent) of David in 1 Chron 16. David had pitched a tent and the Ark of the Covenant was placed in its middle. There were no partitions in it like there were in the Tabernacle of Moses. In this way David was giving us a clearer picture of what worship looks like in heaven. When you are in heaven, you are in the perfect fullness of His love, joy, peace, strength, comfort and everything that He is.

There is another dimension to John 14:1&2 (the Father's house) that I want to expand on. In John 2:13-21, Jesus cleansed the temple for the first time (the second time is recorded in Matt 21:12-17), and the Pharisees asked Him in what authority He was driving out the moneychangers. "Jesus answered them,'Destroy this temple,and in three days I will raise it up'"John 2:19
The people did not understand that He was in actual fact referring to His body and the resurrection.

Jesus came as the physical tent (Tabernacle) of God (Heb 10:5-7). God needed a body on earth to walk amongst His people again (Gen 3:8&9) and for the first time after the fall of man, He could do so through Jesus.

Jesus was the Father's house on earth; all the fullness dwelt in Him (Col 1:19). In John 14:2, Jesus speaks to His disciples about His Father's house having many rooms. He is not referring to the third heaven but to Himself and all the dimensions of the Kingdom that were in Him.

In Christ was the church (the church was established after His resurrection but birthed when His side was pierced on the cross (John 19:34), just as Eve was taken from Adam's side (Gen 2:22)), the gifts, all healing and life, the seven spirits of God, the fullness of the Father, etc. Jesus did not function in the gifts of the Holy Spirit, but in the dimensions of the Spirit. God used Jesus' body to bring all of heaven onto earth whereas Satan used one man's body (Adam) to bring all of hell onto earth; sin, sickness, deception, death, etc (Rom 5:17). In Prov 24:3&4 we read that a house is built by wisdom (earth realm) and that it is established by understanding (heavenly realm) but that it is by knowledge (breaking open of the depths) that the rooms are filled with all kinds of riches (refer to the key of knowledge). Jesus established the heavens, manifested Himself on the earth and revealed the dimensions of the Kingdom to us.

In Matt 16:28 Jesus says that "there are some of those who are standing here who will not taste death until they see the Son of Man coming in His kingdom." He was not referring to His second coming, but to the time after His resurrection. "Some of those standing here" refer to His disciples. Six days after Jesus spoke to his disciples He takes Peter (Faith), James (Hope) and John (Love) with Him up a mountain and He is transfigured (Matt 17:1-9). As Jesus is transfigured they see the dimensions of the Kingdom in Christ. To be able to see the dimensions of the Kingdom we need faith, hope and love, of which these three people are a representation. In verse 9 of this chapter, Jesus says something very 'strange' to these three as they come down the mountain: "…Tell the vision to no one until the Son of Man has risen from the dead."
The reason for this being that no person would understand what Peter, James and John would be trying to explain to him or her, until what they saw in Christ on the mount of transfiguration, was released after Jesus' resurrection.

In John 14:3 Jesus says that He needs to go and prepare a place for the disciples (and all the righteous; past, present and future). This place He was 'going to prepare' was the paradise of man, which up to this time, had not been existent in the third heaven. Hence the 'many rooms' He was referring to could, at this point in time, not be in heaven.

III. Principle #3 – "Hallowed, be Your name": The word 'hallowed' means 'to make holy, to purify or consecrate'. Now God IS holy (1 Pet 1:16) and is therefore calling US to be holy. When we call to Him saying, "Hallowed, be Your name" we are confessing His holiness and at the same time confessing that we need to be holy and pure before our Lord!
In this confession we give God the permission to purify us so that our lives will be acceptable to Him. Remember, not all 'difficulties' are caused by the enemy, as there are times where God is bringing purity and holiness into our lives! At the same time we also acknowledge that His Name is above all names and that He is almighty.

Your relationship with God is not based on what He can do for you but simply on who He IS! Will you love God even if He never DOES anything for you again for the rest of your life from this moment on? The Lord does not deserve your praise, as this requires something to be done on His part, and then in turn you give 'payment' to Him in the form of praise: He is WORTHY of praise!

> "'Your kingdom come. Your will be done,
> On earth as it is in heaven.'"
>
> Matt 6:10

IV. <u>Principle #4</u> – "Your kingdom come. Your will be done": God has a Kingdom and He has a will.

a) It is not about building our own 'kingdom' but about building HIS Kingdom. This Kingdom operates according to certain precepts and principles and it will always operate according to them. We need to come into alignment with this Kingdom and become part of what the Lord is doing and not the other way round! When we give our lives to Christ we also need to adopt the Kingdom culture! People in medieval times lived by the laws of the land that were decreed by the king of that kingdom. The king never lived according to the directions of the people.

b) The Lord has one will but there are three aspects to that will. His will is always good, acceptable and perfect (Rom 12:2):
- His will is good: This word means 'well' and 'beneficial'. It is always beneficial for us when we are in God's will. We do not necessarily always see from God's perspective, and therefore we do not always see the 'good' when God tells us to do something.
- His will is acceptable: It is 'fully agreeable' to the plans and purposes that He has established in our lives before the foundations of the earth. If we stay on the path set for us, we will fulfil all that God has called us to do.
- His will is perfect: God's will is 'complete in various applications of labour, growth, mental and moral character'. There are no imperfections in His will, because He is perfect. There is no such thing as 'God's allowable will' as this would make Him unsure of what He wants us to do. People have used this term as an excuse to cover up for disobedience.

c) As we are obedient to God, He forms and moulds us so that we can fulfil destiny. His Kingdom is *coming* to earth and His will is going to be *done*, whether you will follow His bidding or not, but His plan is to use mankind (Gen 1:26&27)! The choice is yours whether you will be part of it or not.

V. <u>Principle #5</u> – "On earth as it is in heaven": God's Kingdom and will are established and active in the third heaven and we need to establish His Kingdom and will on the earth in exactly the way that it is in the third heaven.

In Gen 1:26-28 we are called to have dominion over the earth. This dominion comes from the third heaven or the Lord's throne room. According to Strong's concordance the word 'dominion' means; to tread down, subjugate[11], to

---

[11] Webster's dictionary: subjugate – to bring under the yoke, under power or dominion, to conquer.

crumble off, (come to, make to) have dominion, prevail against, reign, (bear, make to) rule, (over) take. There are two ways in which we need to have dominion:

a) We are to 'tread down, subjugate, crumble off, have dominion and prevail against' Satan and his fallen angels. We are there to take authority over all the enemy's plots, schemes and dealings on this earth and in the second heaven.
Jesus has given this authority to us but we need to live it through our lives. It will not happen by itself! You need to move Satan out!

b) We are to 'reign, rule, (over) take' on the earth by establishing God's Kingdom on it. We collect from the third heaven where God's Kingdom and will are already established and bring it down onto the earth, taking from heaven and redesigning the earth. We do this by being seated with Christ in heavenly places (Eph 2:6) Who is far above all rule and authority of the enemy (Eph 1:20&21). More detail concerning how this functions is given in chapter seven of this book. God wants us to reign on earth in and through every area of our lives, not just to go to church!

> "Give us this day our daily bread
> And forgive us our debts, as we also have forgiven our debtors"
> Matt 6:11&12

VI. <u>Principle #6</u> – "Give us this day our daily bread": This is not just the physical 'bread' that we need to live, but the very Word that is given to us by the Father. Jesus himself said this when He quoted Deut 8:3 as Satan tempted Him in the wilderness (Matt 4:4; Luke 4:4). The logos (written) word needs to become the rhema (revelation) word in your life. It is only when this happens that the principle of that scripture becomes active in your spirit, and from this point onward you can start applying it. No form of scriptural memory can bring life to your spirit unless the Holy Spirit reveals it to you. If there is no revelation of the word it will result in dead works!

VII. <u>Principle #7</u> – "And forgive us our debts, as we also have forgiven our debtors": This phrase does not only speak of forgiveness, but of the sowing and reaping principle in general, as referred to in Gal 6:7. We need to understand that "what we sow is what we WILL reap" whether it is forgiveness, love, bitterness, money or any other thing; there is no choice in the matter. Jesus uses the topic of forgiveness because it is an important topic. One could actually rephrase this point in the prayer to say 'may what we do (have done) to others come back to us in fullness of measure'!

Remember that every seed that is sown in the natural, will always multiply with the harvest thereof, and the same applies to us in the spirit. There is no seed that does not multiply. However, only God knows how much that seed will multiply. Therefore, we only see the 'fullness of measure' of the seed when it has manifested. Jesus stresses the importance of forgiveness directly after the prayer in Matt 6:14&15.

> "And do not lead us into temptation, but deliver us from evil
> For yours is the Kingdom and the power and the glory forever. Amen"
>
> Matt 6:13

VIII. Principle #8 – "And do not lead us into temptation, but deliver us from evil": We must understand that God does not tempt us but that it is our own lust that entices us (Jam 1:13-15). All temptation is 'common' to man, yours is not 'special', and with every temptation that comes across our way God will give us an escape route (1 Cor 10:13). A very important fact is that temptation in itself is not a sin but a way of escape. As soon as you dwell upon the temptation it becomes sin. Remember that all temptation starts with wrong thinking patterns. This is why it is so important that you renew your mind daily by the rhema word, our daily bread (Rom 12:2) so that your thinking patterns can change. If you think godly thoughts it is more difficult to think sinful thoughts.

IX. Principle #9 – "For yours is the Kingdom and the power and the glory forever. Amen": As mentioned before, the Kingdom belongs to God, but let us bring this part to completion by saying that everything originates and ends in God

a) Everything that He has given to us is not ours, but ours to steward on His behalf. What are you doing with the part of the earth that He has given to you to have 'dominion' over? This includes your business, home, family and friends, finances, etc. Are you being a good steward according to the principles of the Word?

b) What are you doing with the *power* He has entrusted to you? Are you using the gifts of the Spirit correctly? Are you using them at all? There are so many people who do what they do because they want the power and want to be seen by people (pride). In Eze 44:10-16 the Lord clearly says that only the sons of Zadok will be allowed to minister before the Lord. The other Levites who went astray with the rest of Israel will be allowed to do the work of the temple, but they will not be allowed to minister before the Lord. Are you standing before people or before God? He will not tolerate unholy fire to be brought into His presence (2 Chron 26:16-23). God will not give you more power if He cannot trust you.

c) God will not share His *glory* with any one! The Glory is His and His alone. The splendour, worship, praise and honour all belong to Him. He is worthy. An important note at this point is that receiving a compliment is not taking the glory for yourself and is also not pride as long as you thank God for the talent He has given you. When a compliment is given and you say 'it is nothing' you are in actual fact saying that what God has given to you 'is nothing'!

Accept the compliment and praise God for giving you the ability to do what He has given you to do.

B. The revelation of who Christ is[12]

For the next three main points we will be referring to Matt 16:13-19. We all know this scripture, but let us take a closer look to have full understanding thereof. Peter answered the following when Jesus asked who the disciples said He was:
"'You are the Christ, the Son of the living God.'" Matt 16:16

Jesus clearly said that this revelation came from the Heavenly Father, and that it was not something people could know. This is all fine and well, but what does this mean for us today and do we truly understand what Peter said? In this revelation there are five aspects we need to look at and they are: You are; the Christ; the Son; the Living; the God.

I. <u>You are</u> – He is the God in action! In God there is no time. In Gen 1:3-25 we read that God moved in the past, present and future as He created. "God said" speaks of the present; "let there be" speaks of the future, and "there was" speaks of the past. He spoke into the future and the things manifested as if they had already been. God spoke into being all things created out of Whom He is, even your destiny (Gen 1:2; Eph 2:10). Rev 1: 4 says that He IS, He WAS and He WILL BE!
This means that the Lord is always close to you (ever present). He knows your situation and what needs to be done (ever relevant), and He is always there when you call upon Him (always the available One). He has already been in your tomorrow! This is why when God has called you to do a work, all provision is there for you, because God has already completed the work and made provision for you. He now walks with you towards your destiny. At specific intersections in your walk of destiny, you need to access the spirit dimension where the provisions are kept "…for such a time as this" Est 4:14.
Queen Esther was at the right place at the right time. She connected to heaven and through her, a nation was saved! Some may call this a divine appointment, but even if you have a divine appointment you can still miss what God wants to do if you do not connect with heaven and DO YOUR PART, so that God can work what He has determined. Another example in the scripture is 1 Pet 2:24 which says that we were already healed by His stripes. This means that every sickness that there is, already has the healing for it; you just need to access that healing in Christ Jesus!
Phil 4:19 states that "…God will supply all your needs according to His riches in Glory in Christ Jesus".
  a) God will supply: The Lord is the supplier of all things (not your job, bank account, boss, spouse, etc), and He has set all in place so that provision is available at the time you need it.
  b) All your needs: As you move into destiny there are things that are NEEDED so that destiny can be fulfilled. We are not speaking of things we want. These are mere blessings that God gives. Often we see the 'wants' as a greater blessing than the 'needs', but we need to change our perspective on this as it is the 'needs' that allow us to move into destiny.

---

[12] Reference is made to the book "Apostolic Blueprints for Accurate Building" by Dr. Jonathan David.

- c) According to His riches: It is so important to know that God uses His riches to give us supply. His reservoir never runs dry, and all provision, in any form, comes from that reservoir. All was created by Him and all is held together in Him (Col 1:16&17).
- d) In Glory[13]: The word 'glory' in this context means honour, praise and worship, and comes from a base word that means 'to be of reputation'. All honour, praise and worship belong to God alone, not for what He does but for who He is! The Lord is 'of reputation' to do what He has said, and as we bring him all honour, He will establish His Kingdom.
- e) In Christ: We need to be positioned in Christ (a place of being or position) to experience all the fullness that is available to us. I will expand more about being 'in Christ' later.

II. <u>The Christ</u> – Christ means anointed or Messiah. Jesus was the pure and spotless sacrificial Lamb of God. He is the perfect and complete sacrifice and there is no other sacrifice that you can bring (or thing you can do) to make your salvation more complete. Too often we want to substitute the cross and what happened on it with all kinds of things to escape the confrontation of dying to self and surrendering our lives to Christ in its entirety. What happened on the cross is a once off happening. Never again will Jesus need to die for us to deal with our sin and reconcile us to God because "...it is finished!" John 19:30

Every time you want to do something to right your wrong other than repent and 'sin no more', you are literally saying that what Jesus did on the cross was *not good enough* to redeem you to God. In effect you are saying that the work Jesus did was *incomplete.* You need to deal with wrong attitudes concerning your salvation and dying to the 'flesh' as ruthlessly as Christ dealt with your sin on Calvary! The moment you said, "Lord Jesus forgive me for my sin and come and be Lord of my life" you went from sinner to son, from defeated to victorious.

With Christ in our lives we are no longer sinners. It does not make sense to say 'I am a saved sinner'! This concept is not *scriptural.* Rom 8:14-17 says that we have received the spirit of adoption by which we can cry out "Father". The Holy Spirit testifies with our spirit that we are indeed children of the living God. We have been set free from that spirit of slavery which leads to fear and death! Jesus is enough!

III. <u>The Son</u> – There are two main aspects concerning the Son of God:
- a) Jesus is the *only begotten* Son of God (John 3:16). Adam was a son of God (Luke 3:38) just as we are also called sons of God (Rom 8:14&19).

---

[13] Strong's concordance: G1391, doxa, *dox'-ah*, from the base of G1380; glory (as very *apparent*), in a wide application (literally or figuratively, objectively or subjectively): - dignity, glory (-ious), honour, praise, worship.

We are created in the image and likeness of God (Gen 1:26&27) but Jesus is the very imprint of the Father (His DNA); everything that the Father is, He is also. When the disciple Philip asked Jesus to show them the Father, Jesus responded by saying that those who had seen Him had seen the Father (John 14:8&9). When Moses asked God who he should say sent him, God replied, "I AM" (Ex 3:14). Jesus came as 'I AM' revealed. Jesus said this of Himself: I am the bread of life (John 6:35,48,51); I am the light of the world (John 8:12); I am the gate (John 10:7-9); I am the good shepherd (John 10:11&14); I am the resurrection and the life (John 11:25); I am the way and the truth and the life (John 14:6); I am the true vine (John 15:1&5). We need to move away from the concept of being servants of God, because through Christ we have become sons. The Body of Christ needs to raise sons in the church, not just members! They need to raise sons to glory and not just into ministry.

b) Jesus is the *pattern* Son of God (1 Cor 3:11; Eph 2:20). Everything that the church does, and everything that we do as individuals, must be patterned after Christ, and if it is not, you are building wrongly. We cannot add our own ideas and doctrine to the Gospel of the Kingdom. We cannot bend it to make it suit our desires, and we cannot compromise on its principles. Everything in our lives is measured by the corner stone Who is Christ, just as builders used to measure all from the corner stone that was laid in the foundation of a building. If we do not continue in the word that Jesus taught, and if we do not live the principles of the word, we can never have a strong foundation, because He is the foundation and He will not and cannot change. We conform to Him. If the foundation is built incorrectly and is weak, then so too will the rest of the building be. How can you live a victorious live if you do not align yourself to Christ Who is your foundation?

IV. <u>The Living</u> – Christ is not only the begotten and pattern Son of God but He is also the living Son. He was from the beginning of time and He gave life to everything because life was in Him. He is the living Word (John 1:1-5; John 6:68).

When the angel came to Mary and told her that she would be with child, she asked him how this was possible. At his response, Mary said "… may it be done to me according to your word." Luke 1:38
The moment she spoke this, she received the seed of that Living Word! When the Lord speaks a prophetic word to you, you need to lay hold of the seed of that living word. You need to have the eternal Life/Word in your spirit to be able to partake of that prophetic word. If you do not lay hold of the word you will not lay hold of what that word speaks (the fruit and fullness of manifestation)! Once the seed of that word is in your spirit the enemy cannot take it from you no matter what he does, because you are 'impregnated' by it. It is only because of carelessness on your behalf that the word can be 'aborted'. If we look at the lives of Abraham, Joseph, Samuel, Gideon and so many more, we see that they each took hold of the word, and though they went through

different trials they prevailed and saw the Lord bring into fulfilment what He had promised to do. Remember that the Devil will try to steal it, but if you take it, it is in you. Do you truly believe that Jesus is the LIVING and that He brings life to the prophetic words in your life? Then why is it that you do not take hold of the seed of your prophetic word and see it manifest? The word is the seed and your spirit is the soil. You can hear (recognise) the word but not receive (plant) it. It must be planted to grow! We celebrate His death and resurrection, but do we truly believe that He has risen? If we do, why are we then not living in that LIFE which has been made available to us through Him (Phil 3:9-11)? Through Christ we do not just have eternal life, but also the ability to live in His resurrection power and to see Him bring life to the word spoken over us. Jesus Christ is alive for eternity!

V. <u>The God</u> – Jesus is not Mary's little baby boy, born to be King one day. He is already the King of kings and Lord of lords, the absolute, the great and mighty (Phil 2:9-11)! He has risen victorious from the grave and He is seated at the right hand of the Father (Psalm 110:1). On a yearly basis we celebrate the birth of Jesus with the nativity scene of sweet baby boy Jesus as remembrance of the event. Let me ask you this question: "How do you celebrate your birthday?" Do you take out all your baby photos and put them on display for all to see, or do you celebrate the age that you have just become? Is it not time that we celebrate Jesus' birth by rejoicing in who He currently is, Lord and Creator of the universe, and not by remembering Him as a little baby?

In our minds He never grows up because annually He is perceived as a baby. Just a short side note here: Jesus was born around September/October (not December as many assume), at about the time when the Israelites celebrated the Feast of Tabernacles. The significance of this is that Jesus was the Father's house (tabernacle) on earth (refer to John 14:1&2). A coincidence? I should think not! It is God's wholehearted desire to 'tabernacle' with us, and Jesus' birth was a call from the Father to His children: "I am coming to dwell among you".

What is your perspective of God? Do you truly believe that "Now to Him who is able to do far more abundantly beyond all that we ask or think ..." Eph 3:20.
If you believe this and you have met Him as King of Kings, the Victorious One, you can then confront your lion, bear and Goliath; you can even meet 'Pharaoh' and declare to him "let my people go".

C. The church is built on the revelation

"I also say to you that you are Peter, and upon this rock I will build my Church; and the gates of Hades will not overpower it."

Matt 16:18

It is so important to know that Jesus will build His church on the rock, or foundation, of the revelation of Who Christ is and not on Peter, as many have incorrectly assumed! If the body of Christ can grasp this revelation, there will be a revolution that will take place!

I. "You are Peter": When Jesus said, "you are Peter" he was imparting a new identity! In verse 17 Jesus calls Peter "Simon Bar Jona", meaning Simon, son of Jona (John). Jesus firstly says you are blessed Simon, and then in verse 18 He renames him Peter, giving him a new identity in Christ. The very first time Jesus met Simon he said exactly the same thing, "You are Simon the son of John; you shall be called Cephas (Peter)." John 1:42

Jesus repeated the process when Peter received the revelation because he had not yet understood the impartation of identity. Let Christ 'rename' you and impart His identity into your life; your identity is rooted in HIM!

II. "Upon this rock": We need the Holy Spirit to make 'You are; The Christ; The Son; The Living; The God' become alive to us and have Him solidify it in our hearts. If we do not apply this revelation to our lives then there can be no building of His church. As mentioned, the revelation that Peter had is the very foundation that is to be built upon.

III. "I will build": It is Christ Who does the actual building of His church! Is it not interesting how, so often, we want to build the church for God, and then when we have laboured for so long, there are just about no results ("Unless the Lord builds the house, They labour in vain who build it;" Ps 127:1a)? He is the Master Builder and we do only what He tells us to do, just as Jesus did (John 5:19)! If you build for Him you are building your own kingdom in your own strength and it will not stand.

IV. "The gates of Hades will not overpower it": This statement is not meant for 'one day in the future' only, but for NOW as well. We have been called to be a victorious church. It does not mean that there will not be attacks and persecution, but it does mean that we will stand strongly and overcome these persecutions. If the church is living 'You are; The Christ; The Son; The Living; The God', and we allow Christ to be the One who builds the church, then nothing that the enemy does will prevail! So many Christians are living defeated lives but this is not God's plan for them!

D. The keys of the Kingdom of Heaven are for those who function in the revelation

"I will give you the keys of the kingdom of heaven;
and whatever you bind on earth shall have been bound in heaven,
and whatever you loose on earth shall have been loosed in heaven."

Matt 16:19

I. You firstly need to use the Key of knowledge (to unlock the revelations and move in them) in order for you to receive the Keys of the Kingdom of Heaven. "Woe to you lawyers! For you have taken away the key of knowledge; you yourselves did not enter, and you hindered those who were entering." Luke 11:52

As I mentioned in the introduction, there is a great difference between *having* a revelation and actually *functioning* in it! Only those who *function* in the revelation of Who Christ is, actually receive the Keys of the Kingdom of Heaven (the authority to bind and loose)! Very important note: You cannot bind and loose if there is no *righteousness* in your life before God. So many people want to bind and loose things in the spirit but their lives are knowingly in compromise. This in itself disqualifies you, even if you have the revelation. For example: you cannot bind a spirit of addiction if you yourself are under oppression of the same spirit because of an addiction you have, or are not willing to deal with. You need to make right with the Lord and walk in righteousness!

II. "I will give you": Christ is the One who will GIVE you the keys of the Kingdom of Heaven! You cannot just take the keys (authority) to bind and The Key of David loose to use in whichever way you want to. It is for this very reason that so many people are severely attacked and 'trampled underfoot' after doing 'warfare' in the spirit. They bind and loose in what is not given to them.

There are different levels of authority that are released to us according to our relationship with God. In our relationship with God, there are different levels of revelation which we receive the closer we move towards Him, and as our sensitivity in hearing His voice increases (John 5:19). Authority is entrusted to us.

What level of authority have you been given to function in? Identify it and function in that until God takes you to another level.

III. "The keys of the Kingdom of Heaven": This clearly states that there is a kingdom involved. Refer to principle number 4 and 5 in point 'A'.

IV. "Heaven": Throughout verse 19 the word 'heaven' is referring to the third heaven or throne room of God (ouranos), and not the second heaven (epouranios)! We have simply had an incorrect understanding of which 'heaven' the scripture is speaking about, and therefore act according to that wrong understanding. How can you bind and loose things on earth and see the manifestation thereof in the throne room of God? If this 'heaven' then refers to the throne room of God, we need to look a little deeper to gain full understanding of how binding and loosing actually works as detailed in this scripture.

V. "Whatever you bind/loose on earth shall have been bound/loosed in heaven": Many people believe that when they pray and bind/loose here on earth, the principalities, etc. will be bound in the heavenlies (second heaven). This assumption is incorrect if in fact it is standing on its own, and also *one* of the reasons why we do not see 'results' when we pray. What Jesus is actually saying here is that when we pray, He will enable us to see into the third heaven and seeing and hearing what God has already bound/loosed in the decree He has spoken from HIS THRONE, we speak out the same, and the manifestation thereof comes. This means that just as Jesus only did what He saw the Father do, so we are to also do only what we see Him do (John 5:19&30; John 8:38). The word says in Ephesians 5:1 that we are to be imitators of God. Notably this 'imitating of God' is not just meant in the current context but is to be applied in every area of our lives.

Important notes:
a) You can only 'see' into the third heaven if you are 'seated with Christ in heavenly places' (Eph 2:6). You cannot see from the earth into the third heaven! You need to be spiritually positioned 'far above all rule and

authority with Christ' (Eph 1:20&21). To be seated with Christ in heavenly places requires relationship and this is detailed further when we talk about the different dimensions of the key of David.

b) The decrees God gives us to speak will be according to the authority He has given us.

c) Whatever you bind/loose has already been done (past tense) in the throne room. You are now echoing it, and by that, establishing His Kingdom and will on earth (Matt 6:10)! The Lord makes us part of His plan and we work with Him.

d) The manifestation of the decree that you make will affect the second heaven (spirit realm – the principalities and powers) firstly, and then manifest itself into the first heaven (physical realm). This may happen directly after the declaration is made, or some time after.

The keys of the Kingdom of Heaven are used in conjunction with the Key of David How this functions will be explained later.

APPLICATION STUDY GUIDE FOR CHAPTER ONE

1. What principles, taught in Chapter One, do you not understand or only partially understand? Take as much time as you need and ask the Holy Spirit to break open all aspects. If necessary, read the chapter or those parts of the chapter that you are uncertain about again.
2. Which of the four aspects of 'the Keys of the Kingdom of Heaven' does God want to establish in your spirit at this point in time? What are you going to do so that these revelations will remain part of your life?
   a. The revelation of nine principles of the Kingdom of Heaven.
   b. The revelation of who Christ is.
   c. The church is built on the revelation.
   d. The keys of the Kingdom of Heaven are for those who function in the revelation.
3. Study the following scriptures:
   a. Matt 13:10-17 and Matt 18:3
      - Have you been at a place in your walk with God that has been more intense than now? Why have you stagnated in your relationship; what has been 'taken away'?
      - Has the Lord been speaking to you about changing things in your life, but you have not responded to His prompts? Do you see but not perceive?
      - What are YOU going to do about it?
   b. 1 Peter 4:12-14
      - Jesus never said that things would be easy! If we understand who Christ is we will be able to stand strong because He Who is in us is stronger than anything else in the world (1 John 4:4)! In what areas of your life do you fear because you have not surrendered them to Christ?
      - What are you going to do about it?

Pray with me:

"Lord, open my heart to You again. Please forgive me for becoming passive in my walk with You, and help me, by Your Spirit, to take responsibility for what I need to do in my relationship with You.

Father open my ears to hear and my eyes to see, that I may walk in the path You have set for me. I want to surrender … (name what you want to surrender) … to You. I declare that You are the source of all things. Give me grace Lord Jesus to live a surrendered life. Amen."

CHAPTER TWO

RESTORING THE TABERNACLE OF DAVID

Psalm 122 verse one speaks of a joyful occasion as people are called to come to the house of the Lord.

> "I was glad when they said to me,'Let us go to the house of the Lord.'"

But what does it mean to come to the house of the Lord? God is restoring His House and calling all of His sons (women are as much sons of God as men are part of the bride of Christ) from every tribe, tongue and nation to come into His presence. His desire is to gather us to break off all limitations from His people.

We have already discovered that keys speak of authority over something, and therefore if you have a key, you have authority in that area. The big problem we have, though, is that we do not have all the authority available to us to move into every area that we need to. If we did, we would not need each other; or God, for that matter.

[1]All nations are of one blood (Gen 1:28; Acts 17:26) and God's intention is that we may exercise the dominion He has given us. Unfortunately, because of selfish ambition, pride and a fallen nature, people wanted to gather and reach into heaven, and make a name for themselves (being connected to the wrong source), so that they would not be scattered (Gen 11:4). This desire went directly against the command of the Lord who said in Gen 1:28 that mankind was to multiply and fill the earth. The reason for this being that God wants to establish His kingdom over the whole earth and not just one part of it. God confused the people's language at the tower of Babel (Gen 11:1-9) to force them to move away from each other and fill the earth. God further had to divide the people to limit what they do because they were drawing from the wrong source (Satan) and standing unified, they would be able to do whatever they set their mind to do. With the confusion at Babel, there was a division of authority that the people had. All people had authority over different areas but not one tribe had authority over all.

After the resurrection of Christ, atonement had been made between man and God and at Pentecost (Acts 1:8; Acts 2:1-4) the Holy Spirit was poured out over mankind. Now there was a call to unite in Christ (in the spirit) so that His body could function without limitation! So we see that at Babel there was division to disperse and limit, and at Pentecost the Spirit was poured out to unite (gather); to bring fullness with no limitation. We are now reconnected to the correct source being God, because of Christ, and we can now start to function in the original task given to us, namely to establish His Kingdom. In Acts 15:15-18 (reference made to Amos

---

[1] Reference in these paragraphs is made to the teaching on DVD "The Key of David" by Rev. Michael Pitts. So 'tabernacle' refers to the coming together and dwelling in the presence of the Lord. Let us take a closer look at Psalm 122 to discover the fullness of what is said above.

9:11) it says that God will rebuild and restore the Tabernacle of David. This is not merely referring to the restoration of worship in the church as is so often mentioned and assumed, but to the full restoration and implementation of the authority given to us as we *come together* (Tabernacle of David) in the house of the Lord flowing in the *dimensions* that David functioned in (the key of David).

> "I was glad when they said to me,'Let us go to the house of the Lord.'"
>
> Ps 122:1

1. "I was glad/go to the house": Now is the time when God is rebuilding David's tabernacle. You need to come to the house of the Lord and tabernacle in the house of the Lord.
    I. Firstly you need to understand that He is Lord of the house! You can be in the House of the Lord (church) and not have Him Lord of the House! It is God's house and we need to abide by the 'rules' of His house. Although we are sons in His household, we cannot just do what we please, as there are principles that we need to function in. There is an order to the way we conduct a service. Unfortunately, the way we act in the house of the Lord has made Him feel unwelcome in His house!
    II. Secondly you must understand that the 'house of the Lord' is a place of dwelling (Ps 23:6). To dwell[2] means to sit down or to remain. We come together in the house of the Lord because we are united through Christ. Unfortunately we do not understand the true meaning of unity: So often Ps 133:1 is quoted incorrectly when there is a pastor's fellowship or churches working together on a project. To say this is unity is a grave mistake! Let us come to a point of understanding on this 'unity': The word brothers or brethren[3] speaks of being like or of kindred spirit, so to say, coming from the same womb or father. True unity can therefore only be achieved when all parties involved are connected to or drawing from the same source, have the same revelation about what is to be done, and all function in the area that they have authority over!

By coming together in unity like this, the oil (anointing) will flow from the head (Christ) down to the body (those in unity) and the Lord's blessing will be upon them to do the work (Ps 133:2&3).

---

[2] Strong's concordance: H3427; yâshab, *yaw-shab'*: A primitive root; properly to sit down (specifically as judge, in ambush, in quiet); by implication to *dwell*, to *remain*; causatively to *settle*, to *marry*. -(make to) abide (-ing), continue, (cause to, make to) dwell (-ing), ease self, endure, establish, X fail, habitation, haunt, (make to) inhabit (-ant), make to keep [house], lurking, X marry (-ing), (bring again to) place, remain, return, seat, set (-tle), (down-) sit (-down, still, -ting down, -ting [place] -uate), take, tarry.

[3] H251, 'âch, *awkh*. A primitive word; a *brother* (used in the widest sense of literal relationship and metaphorical affinity or resemblance (like H1)): -another, brother (-ly), kindred, like, other. Compare also the proper names beginning with "Ah-" or "Ahi-". In Greek G80 Adelphos or Adelphoi. H1, 'âb, awb. A primitive word; father in a literal and immediate, or figurative and remote application: -chief, (fore-) father ([-less]), X patrimony, principal. Compare names in "Abi-"

> "Our feet are standing within your gates, O Jerusalem, Jerusalem, that is built as a city that is compact together;"
>
> Ps 122:2&3

2. This 'Jerusalem' is not just referring to the physical city but to the spiritual 'Jerusalem' in you! David brought the Ark of the Lord, being a symbol of God's presence, back to Jerusalem, which is the holy city. Sacrifices were made while the procession was in progress (2 Sam 6:12-14), which symbolises living under the blood covering of Christ. Once in the city, David sets up twenty four hour worship to take place around the Ark, as the work required it (1 Chron 16:4&37-42). The word clearly states in 1 Cor 3:16 and 1 Cor 6:19 that our bodies are a temple for the Holy Spirit. In John 4:19-24 Jesus tells the Samaritan woman that there will come a time when worship will not take place in Jerusalem anymore, because the Father is not looking for a physical place we can worship from, but for a person who will worship Him! If we are the temple of God, then the place where we worship 'from' is our spirit. This means that we are not confined to go somewhere to worship, although at the same time it does not give us reason to 'stay away from church', because the word is clear that we should not neglect the fellowship of believers. Our 'feet' (position) are standing inside 'the gates' (a place of dwelling and refuge). Hebrews 12:22-24 declares that we have come to Mount Zion and the heavenly Jerusalem. 'Zion' always refers to the church, being either militant or victorious (in this case victorious) and 'Jerusalem' speaks of an attribute[4] not a location. You are a 'holy city' for the Lord. The word 'compact' in Ps 122:3 literally means 'to have fellowship with, join self or together'. As we come together God will dwell in the praises of his people (Ps 22:3, 2 Chron 5:13&14). We are a greater 'tabernacle' for God when we come together in unity. The greater the unity, the greater the presence of God, and the more intense the corporate anointing that is released upon the people (again Ps 133). Note that praise comes before the dwelling!

> "To which the tribes go up, even the tribes of the Lord -
> An ordinance for Israel - to give thanks to the name of the Lord,
> For there thrones were set for judgement, The thrones of the house of David."
>
> Ps 122:4&5

3. [5]Every tribe, tongue and nation has something to bring as they come to the house of the Lord. There is a land that needs to be possessed but it will only be possessed if all come together. Jacob prophesied over his sons and each had an authority over something (Gen 49:1-27). When they took the Promised Land they conquered it as a nation, a united Israel, but all received a part of the land. You don't possess the whole land by yourself; only parts of it, but all together you possess the land.

---

4 Webster's dictionary: That which is attributed: a quality or property inseparable from anything.
"To which the tribes go up, even the tribes of the Lord – An ordinance for Israel – to give thanks to the name of the Lord, For there thrones were set for judgement, The thrones of the house of David."
Ps 122:4&5

5 Reference in this point is made to the teaching on DVD "The Key of David" by Rev. Michael Pitts.

So you bring to the house of the Lord (church) what you have authority over; you must have a crown before you can cast it down (Rev 4:10) and God becomes King of kings and sets up a threshold (bind and loose) to make decrees (judgement). Keep in mind that 'thrones' speak of plural rulership. Now it may sometimes happen that there are not enough thrones and you cannot make a decree over a specific situation. For example: If all are suffering under the yoke of a spirit of poverty, all are bound and there is then no authority; but, if some have overcome, there is faith and the spirit is broken.

Note that there needs to be righteousness in the way we live to be able to render decrees, and the people who are suffering need to align themselves to God's Word so that the enemy cannot attack them again. Heb 11:13-16 speaks about people receiving a promise from the Lord and although they did not take possession of it in the physical they saw beyond the physical and took possession of what was beyond (the spiritual reward/land). Do not just focus on the 'now' but look beyond that so that you may receive the fullness!

> "Pray for the peace of Jerusalem: May they prosper who love you. May peace be within you walls, and prosperity within your palaces."
>
> Ps 122:6&7

4. If there is 'peace within your walls' it means that you are at peace within your spirit. It is a place of no turmoil and of rest! If there is peace in your spirit God will cause you to prosper in all you do! Remember that prosperity is not just about physical things, but about your entire being. Prosperity primarily comes from within and not from the outside; prosper in your spirit and the physical prosperity will follow.

> "For the sake of my brothers and my friends, I will now say,
> 'May peace be within you.'
> For the sake of the house of the Lord our God,
> I will seek your good."
>
> Ps 122:8&9

5. It is when the body comes together that the corporate anointing is released (Ps 133:1&2)! We are to ensure the peace of our fellow believers and not criticise and judge them. The Lord expects us to correct, but in love and not in judgment (2 Tim 3:16&17)! If Jesus forgave them their sins who are we to judge them if they turn to Him in repentance.

If there is to be the full restoration of the Tabernacle of David, *the Lord's body needs to come together* to 'tabernacle' or dwell in His House so that He can come and inhabit His people: God's people in His house and God in His people (Isa 66:1)!

APPLICATION STUDY GUIDE FOR CHAPTER TWO

Before we start with the actual application part for chapter two I would like to share a little more concerning the 'dwelling' we need to come to. In one of the most famous Psalms, Psalm 23, David gives us insight as to how we get to dwell in the 'house of the Lord'.

a) "The Lord is my Shepherd, I shall not want." Ps 23:1
We all know that there is only one 'Lord' of creation, but before you can dwell with Him you need to know Him. 'My' speaks of being personal, and that is what makes God different from any other 'god' or idol. He wants to be involved in your whole life and does not want someone else to mediate between you and Him. He is a personal God. A 'shepherd' is someone who gives guidance, protection, discipline, security and meets your needs (not wants). 'Not want' indicates you will not need or lack anything, as God gives what is needed physically, emotionally and spiritually; all areas of your life are covered. You will not be in distress and need have no fear of needing guidance, protection, discipline, security and food because He is there.

b) "He makes me lie down in green pastures; He leads me beside quiet waters." Ps 23:2
'He makes' and 'He leads' indicates that it is God who brings you to/leads you into destiny as you surrender to Him. He 'makes' or creates the dream He has for you, but He is also the one who 'leads' or guides you in that dream. 'Lie down' speaks of a position of rest in God. This comes from being 'in' Christ and is a position in the spirit (Matt 28:19). See chapter three for more detail on this point. 'Green pastures' refers to a place of growth and sustenance whereas 'quiet waters' speak of the Holy Spirit's gentle but steady working in your life, causing you to be refreshed. Rivers flow in a certain direction. There is an increase in the 'water level' in our spirits because of the Holy Spirit's working.

c) "He restores my soul; He guides me in the paths of righteousness for His name's sake." Ps 23:3
'Restores my soul' speaks of the renewing of the mind (Rom 12:2). It is only when we come to the place where we allow the Holy Spirit to work in our lives that we can start to read the word of God in a different way. If God 'guides' us in paths it means that, for that guidance to take place, there is instruction given and carried out. Together with this, there must be application of discipline and consequence if we are disobedient to the guidance. This guidance takes place so that we can walk in 'paths of righteousness', which merely refers to be in a relationship of right standing with God. We need to apply the principles the Lord has revealed to us, not because of doing them to please Him, but because they have become part of our daily lives as our minds are renewed. God does all things for 'His name's sake'. He is worthy of all the glory and we are to reflect that glory wherever we go. The people should see Christ and not us.

d) "Even though I walk through the valley of the shadow of death, I fear no evil, for You are with me; Your rod and Your staff, they comfort me." Ps 23:4

Firstly we need to understand that we will walk through 'the valley of the shadow of death'. There will be times when difficulties, trials and attacks come our way! What we need to have revelation of though, is that whatever we experience, no matter how bad it is, it is only a shadow of death and not death itself! The enemy wants us to believe his lies, but we need to know that he is conquered because of Christ; through the life of Christ He conquered the works of the enemy; through His death He conquered the power of the enemy and through His resurrection He conquered the fear of death. 'Death' does not just speak of physical death but of anything that causes fear to enter into our lives. If we can fully grasp the fact that all power of the enemy is declared null and void (unless we live in the flesh/sin) through Christ, then we will also recognise that whatever the enemy brings to us is only a 'shadow' to cause us to fear again.

As soon as we allow fear into our lives we are no longer living with the spirit of adoption, which brings freedom (Rom 8:15). Once we have understood this we will then 'fear no evil' because God is with us no matter what the situation. Also notice that we will not fear because we are walking in paths of righteousness with God and therefore He is continually with us. Righteousness comes before walking without fear. The Lord's 'rod' is there to keep wild animals (the enemy) at bay. The closer you are to Jesus the more difficult it becomes for the enemy to attack you because you are walking with the Shepherd. The 'staff' was used to bring sheep back, and for discipline. Discipline never seems good at the time it is given, but it is always beneficial to us and gives us the security that the Father cares.

e) *"You prepare a table before me in the presence of my enemies; You have anointed my head with oil; My cup overflows." Ps 23:5*
God will 'prepare a table' before us which speaks of covenant (Heb 13:20) and fellowship with Him. Our God is a covenant maker. From the beginning of time it was God who came to make a covenant with man, not the other way around! The first covenant was made with man who was to rule over the earth (Gen 1:26-31), the second with Noah (Gen 6:18; Gen 9:9-17) and the third was the covenant with Abram (Gen 15:18). The new covenant was with us through Christ (Heb 13:20&21) but every time it is God Who initiates the covenant because He is a covenant God.

God will confirm this covenant with us in the 'presence of our enemies' to put our enemies to shame; our enemies become His enemies and His enemies become our enemies because of the covenant. He will bring us to a place of strength in Him before our enemies and they will be powerless (Zech 3:1-10) because we are in covenant with the loving God.

'Anoint my head with oil' declares that we are set apart for God's use. We do not just have an anointing; He has become our anointing. This means that we do not just function when we 'feel' the anointing, but we move according to His leading all the time! As we follow Christ's leading we will lead (head) others (leadership in Christ). A pouring out of our very lives in His Kingdom now takes place as our 'cup overflows' because we are a vessel for God's use, overflowing to the people. What you have, what God has given you is not your own: it is for others!

f) "Surely goodness will follow me all the days of my life, and I will dwell in the house of the Lord forever." Ps 23:6

Now 'goodness and love will follow' because of the outpouring of our lives; wherever we go and whatever we do, it will cause the goodness and love of God to flow. The 'follow' comes because we first pour out and then only will you see the goodness and love manifest! From this point we come to the place where we 'dwell' which speaks of the habitation or residence, a staying in God and the 'House of God' (The Father's house has many 'rooms' or dimensions (John 14:2); see chapter one page 17). 'Forever' does not just refer to eternity, but firstly speaks of a continual living in Christ while we are still on earth. If we live in Christ on earth we will also live with Him forever!

QUESTIONS

1. Do you fully understand the terms 'coming together' and 'dwelling' of which is spoken in this chapter? Allow the Holy Spirit to solidify these principles in your mind and spirit by:
   a. Reading the chapter or parts of the chapter that you are uncertain about again.
   b. Studying the following scripture:
      - Acts 2:41-44
2. You need to come to a local body where you can fellowship and grow, and most importantly, live out your destiny that God has set inside you. Answer the following about the body you fellowship at:
   a. Are you there because you are comfortable and not challenged?
   b. Are you passive in following what God has given you to do (your destiny)?
   c. Are you a burden to the pastor because you are not allowing the vision of the 'House' to be birthed and activated in your spirit? If you have answered 'yes' to any of the above questions you need to seriously evaluate your position in the body of Christ and need to make some drastic changes accordingly:
      a. You are to allow the Lord to challenge you in your life. A church that only teaches what soothes the ears will never have spiritual growth. Do not allow yourself to be part of a Laodicean church that is lukewarm (Rev 3:14-22) for God will surely spit you out!
      b. You need to be active in your walk with God in the church where you are. What can you do to be of 'service' in the church? Do not just serve in the church because you have a title of leadership, but lead because of what God has placed in you.
      c. You need God to show you to which part of the body you need to connect. Remember that God places you in a church because the destiny that you are to live will enable the pastor to fulfil the vision that God has given him. Too often we want to run outside the church with our own 'ministry' in isolation, instead of functioning as part of a specific body

in unity. Remember that once you have come to a church of which God has said 'this is where you fit in my body', do not get up and run away at the first conflict! Work through the issues because if you leave you will firstly be moving away from the will of God, and secondly the 'issues' will follow you to where you go because YOU have the issues!

3. How can YOU 'dwell' more effectively in the Lord's presence? Ask the Lord to show you what you need to do and then start implementing it in your life.

Pray with me:

"Lord teach me to dwell in your presence so that I may receive the fullness of life that you have for me. Lord Jesus, forgive me where I have neglected You and the fellowship of your body; where I have separated myself from your communion.

I come to You and ask that you will position me in your body so that I may function as a living stone to glorify You! Amen."

CHAPTER THREE

THE KEY OF DAVID: POSITION AND DIMENSIONS

Allow me to start this chapter by giving you the definitions of the words 'position' and 'dimension' from the Webster's Dictionary, so that you are able to have a better insight concerning these two words and their application in the following chapters.
Position: situation; place occupied; disposition; arrangement (with relation to other things); posture; state of affairs; ground taken in; argument or dispute; principle laid down; place in society; official employment.
Dimension: measure in length, breadth and thickness (the three dimensions of space as understood in Euclidean geometry); extent; size.
Dimensional: concerning dimension (one two or three dimensional space = space of one, two or three dimensions).

What position?
Everything that we do is to flow from out of a position or standing of being 'in' Christ. In Matt 28:19 Jesus gives us the command to make disciples of all nations and then to baptise them into the name of the Father, Son and Holy Spirit. This scripture does not just refer to the baptism in water but to a spiritual baptism in the Lord. The word baptise comes from the Greek word baptid'zo which literally means to submerge. The best way to demonstrate this word would be by taking a white cloth and submerging it into purple dye. When the cloth is taken out again it will be purple and not white anymore because it has been saturated with the purple pigments. We are not called merely to submerge ourselves in water, which is a public confession of our faith in Christ, but to 'submerge' ourselves in Christ so that all He is can emanate through us.

We are mainly focussed on the baptism of the Holy Spirit (Acts 1:8; 1 Cor 3:16), which is a necessity because He is the One Who gives us the nine gifts of the Spirit and the power to function in them. However, we need to take one step further to be in Christ so that we can have the fullness of life. Acts 17:28 says: "for in Him we live and move and exist ..." which clearly says that all life source is in Christ and therefore we need to position ourselves *in* Him. This reflects the exact same relation that Jesus and the Father had as we read in John 14:10 "Do you not believe that I am in the Father, and the Father is in me?"

This concept is further detailed in John 15:1-11 where Jesus speaks of being the vine (the core of life) and we are the branches (the expression of Him). Jesus says that if we abide[6] in Him we will bear good fruit and He will do whatever we ask for. This leads us to ask a vital question: "If Jesus tells us that if we ask Him anything in His name He will give it to us, why is it that we do not receive what we ask for?" (John 14:11-15; John 15:16; John 16:23&24). There can only be one of

---

6   Webster's Dictionary: dwell or stay, remain in a place, endure.

two reasons: Jesus was not being completely open about what He said OR we are missing a principle that Jesus was teaching His disciples. As Jesus always reveals the truth the answer is simple; we are the ones who must be missing a principle!

The principle is this: "In the name of Jesus" is not a mere phrase that we are to 'add on' after each prayer to make sure that what we have asked for, is asked 'in His name' but 'in His name' is a position **from which** we ask God to release His will in our lives and on the earth!

If we are *positioned in Christ* we can *know His will* or destiny for our lives; if we know His will and ask Him to do it, He will *always grant* what we have asked for, without exception, because what we have asked is His will and desire (1 John 5:14&15).
This principle is further founded in 2 Cor 5:17 where 'in Christ' we are a new creature (also see Eph 2:10). Let us do away with the cliché "in Jesus name" after our prayers, and rather live our whole lives positioned 'in Him', as He was in the Father!
Christ is in us and we are in Christ, just as Jesus is in the Father and the Father is in Jesus. Once we have grasped the concept of being 'in' Christ we can move to the next level – dimensions in our positions 'in' Him.

What dimension/s?
To understand dimensions pertaining to the key of David we need to firstly understand what David's role or 'job description' was. There are three areas in which David functioned, namely that he was a king, a priest and a prophet. Further we need to realise that it was not just something David did; it was a dimension in the spirit in which he functioned.

David as Priest:
- David was a shepherd boy when he learned to worship the Lord (1 Sam 16:11&18). David could bear his heart to God in every situation because he knew God at an intimate level and this can be clearly seen in the Psalms. David's communication with God was truly powerful, so much so, that the times when he did not consult God and made mistakes because of this, he was quick to repent. By reading the prayer in 2 Sam 7:18-29 we clearly see David's heart toward the Lord. Note that in verse eighteen it says that David went to *sit* before the Lord; what awesome relationship!
- David presented the sacrifice before the Lord (2 Sam 6:17&18; 2 Sam 24:18-25), something that only a priest can do.
  We read throughout the Old Testament that where kings wanted to bring a sacrifice to God, He judged them: Saul's sacrifice was not accepted -1 Sam 13:9-14; Uzziah's sacrifice was not accepted -2 Chron 26:16-21; David was an exception as he brought numerous sacrifices to the Lord -2 Sam 6:12&13; 2 Sam 24:21-25.
- As a priest you can come into a place of vulnerability and transparency (2 Sam 6:20-22). God 'covered' David's vulnerability and transparency by judging Michal, the daughter of Saul, as she despised her husband in his relationship

with the Lord (2 Sam 6:16&23).
- In a place of worship the enemy must leave (1 Sam 16:23).
- In a place of worship you are protected (1 Sam 18:10-12).

David as Prophet:
- David was a shepherd boy when he learned to function as a prophet. •
- David displayed a prophetic preview of the restoration of relationship the way that God had intended it to be from the beginning. The tent of David (1 Chron 16:1-4, 37-42) was a prophetic preview of the worship we see depicted in Revelation 4. All is centred round the throne of God. It is also a prophetic preview of the access we have to God through the death and resurrection of Christ. The tent of David had no partitions in the way that the Tabernacle of Moses or the Temple had. The Ark of the Covenant was placed in the centre of the tent and the Levites worshiped around it. When Jesus died, the veil of the temple was torn, breaking the division between the Holy of Holies and the holy place symbolising that all can now enter in.

David as King:
- David was a shepherd boy when he learned to rule as a king in his jurisdiction. He not only tended the sheep, but also fought against the lion and the bear to protect them (1 Sam 17:33-37).
- David was anointed king and his rule extended over the land (2 Sam 2:4; 2 Sam 5:3&4). David took back what had been taken by the Philistines (2 Sam 5:17-25).
- David was in God's favour and his rule increased (2 Sam 5:10; 2 Sam 6:8-17).

Bringing the two together:
From this we can see that David was positioned 'in' the Lord and functioned in three dimensions. When we speak about the 'key of David' (Rev 3:7) and the ability to *function* therein, we are speaking of *having the authority* (because of our position in Christ) to function in these dimensions of a king, a priest and a prophet. Every Christian is to function in these dimensions, not just a selected few!

Each of these dimensions is expressed in Rev 5:1-10 (read this scripture). Before we explore the dimensions in more detail, let us take a look at the expression of these dimensions through the God Head. Keep in mind that according to Gen 1:26-28:
- God created man a spirit being in the same category as Himself. We are God's kind and therefore man is a spirit being. (Gen 2:7). Our mind, will and emotions determine the life that God has placed in us (through Christ) to pass out or to be cut off.
- Man is created in the image and likeness of God. The 'image' speaks of the inward spirit potential that we have, that is, all that God is, and the 'likeness' refers to the potential of our character to express Him, in other words, the outward expression of God.

We see that:
1) *God the Father* is our **King** (Matt 6:10, 1 Tim 1:17, Rev 15:3). His Kingdom is established in the third heaven. Refer also to Chapter one page eighteen.
2) *Jesus, the Son*, is our high **Priest** (Heb 4:14; Heb 5:5).
3) *The Holy Spirit* is the **Prophet** (Acts 28:25).

Referring to our scripture in Proverbs 3:19&20 again and taking into further consideration that when Jesus was transfigured on the mountain, He took with him Peter (faith), James (hope) and John (love), each representing a further expansion of these dimensions, note the following:

1) The **earth** was founded by the Lord's **wisdom** and this speaks of the dimension of the **King**. Keep in mind that God's Kingdom IS already established in heaven. It is a necessity that a king rules his kingdom with wisdom so that the fullness of what he wants to establish can be manifest in that kingdom and in his subjects. Together with **wisdom** you need to operate with **love**. If your kingdom is operated by dictatorship the people will stir up a revolt but if it is operated in love, being the most important of the three (hope, faith and love), there will be grace and discipline. God loved us so much that he sent Jesus to redeem us to Himself (John 3:16; John 14:20-23; Eph 6:23; 1 Thess 1:3, 1 John 2:15; 1 John 3:1). Love is represented by the colour gold, which speaks of purification, trial by fire, God's glory, royalty, kingship and divinity (Ex 37:6-7; Ps 19:9&10; Ps 119:126-128; Heb 9:3-5; Rev 1:16; Rev 21:18, 23). We need to have a pure, godly love flowing through us to people.
2) The **heavens** were established by the Lord's **understanding** and this represents the dimension of the **priest**. A priest has the ability to bring forth understanding in relationship with God and he has the ability to touch God's heart. With **understanding** also comes **hope**. Hope is released as we understand the deeper truths of God. Without hope the people will perish (1 Thess 1:3; Col 1:27; Tit 2:11-14).
Hope is represented by the colour silver, which speaks of redemption, innocence, truth and God's words (Ex 21:32; Ex 30:11-16, Ps 12:6; Matt 27:3-7; John 17:17; Rom 3:24). We carry the message of redemption and the truth of God's word to set man free.
3) The **depths** are broken up by His **knowledge** and this refers to the dimension of the **prophet**. A prophet has the ability to see what the Lord sees and can declare the words of the Lord, which in turn produces **faith**. Your faith is stirred because your destiny is revealed! (Acts 6:5, 11:24, Gal 3:1-14, Jude 1:20). The colour bronze/brass/copper represents faith, which is a symbol of judgment upon sin, fires of testing, endurance and strength (Ex 30:18; Ex 38:8; Deut 33:25; Eze 1:7; Rev 1:15). Our faith needs to be able to stand any testing that the enemy brings against us and we need to endure till the end!

- Note: read Gal 5:4-6 and see how hope, faith and love 'work' together.

Jesus was tempted in all things by which man is tempted (Heb 2:17&18; Heb 4:15), and therefore his redemption for us is complete. Jesus went through the same temptation that Adam and Eve went through in Gen 3:1-5. We can see from Matt 4:3-10, that it is in these dimensions in which Satan has lost power and authority to operate. Satan tempted Adam and Eve just after they were created (revealed on the earth) and before they could bring their dominion into its fullness. In the very same way Jesus was tempted just after He was revealed (baptised and appointed by the Father) and before He started His ministry (dominion on earth). Let us look at this parallel:

1) In Gen 3:1-4 Adam and Eve were told to 'eat from the fruit' for they would 'surely not die', and Jesus was told to 'change these stones into bread' (Matt 4:3). Both these instances make reference to the **kingly dimension** or *rulership* that Satan was attacking.
   - Satan wanted man to function from a perverted source of authority: rebellion. We need to function in the correct authority given to us by Christ (our daily bread from Him; Matt 4:4) and not misuse what He has given us to our own gain or purpose. Man's kingly authority was stripped because he received instruction from a perverted source, bringing death in his spiritual ability to lead and live by God's rule.
   - Jesus was tested on His Kingly authority by Satan (a perverted source) trying to get Him to listen to instructions. Had He obeyed the voice of deception, His integrity and authority to rule would have been nullified.
   - In the world system today, Satan allows people to *rule* with money: the more money, the more ability to influence, manipulate and control. You can only accept mastership of one god; either the Lord of Hosts or the god Mammon (Matt 6:21&24).
   - Jesus was bought with thirty pieces of silver (Matt 26:14-16), and therefore He has gained authority over everything that can be 'bought' and controlled with money; the tool to rule in Satan's kingdom.
   - When Jesus answers Satan, He reminds him of the true Source of authority, being God (Matt 4:4). Jesus came and restored our kingly authority (Matt 28:18-20).

2) Adam and Eve were told that they would 'be like God, knowing good and evil' (Gen 3:5) and in Matt 4:6 it was said that Jesus should 'throw [Himself] down if He were 'the Son of God' and promised that if He would 'worship' Satan, all would be His (Matt 4:8-10). Both of these instances refer to the **priestly dimension** or *relationship* that was attacked by Satan.
   - The enemy's aim was to target selfishness and lust, which comes about when we want anything outside of God and Who He is. This is called idolatry, and the result is separation from God – eternal death. Man's priestly function was stripped away. We will only lust after other things if our relationship is not secure in the Lord. Do not test God's patience by 'flirting' with idols (Matt 4:7). You need to 'die' to selfishness and move in the spirit. Satan wanted to trick man in thinking that we could know all as created beings. God moves us into progression of revelation, and although we are created in His image and likeness, we can never be God or know all. Joshua told Israel to choose whom they wanted to serve, but he and his household chose the Lord (Josh 24:15).
   - Jesus' priestly function was tested by Satan trying to get Him to test or

'tempt' God on His word and also to bow down to him (Satan). Jesus came to reconcile man with God in relationship, and had He failed, His role as the High Priest would have been cancelled.
- In the world system today Satan allows people to break out of relationship with God by bringing in sexual desires and self-gratification (idolatry). The more sexual perversions you succumb to, the deeper you move into idolatry (Rom 6:12&13; 1 Cor 10:14).
- Jesus was in constant relationship with the Father but on the cross He went through separation so that we may be reconciled (John 14:9-11, Mark 15:34).
- Jesus restored our priesthood (1 Peter 2:9).

3) Adam and Eve were told that their 'eyes [would] be opened' (Gen 3:5) whereas Jesus was shown 'all the kingdoms of the world' and promised that if He would 'worship' Satan all would be His (Matt 4:8-10). Both these instances refer to the **prophetic dimension** or *revelation* that the enemy was attacking.
- In God's presence things will be revealed (Matt 4:10) and it is that revelation that Satan seeks to cut so that we are kept in darkness. If we have revelation of Who Christ is and move in that revelation, the enemy will not be able to rule in or through us. Man's prophetic role was stripped from him.
- Jesus was tested on His prophetic calling by Satan trying to show Him a 'shorter way' to obtain all the kingdoms of the earth, which was only a part of what God saw. All the earth belongs to God anyway (Ps 24:1), but God's Kingdom consists of much more, and if He had taken a short cut, Jesus would only have had a part. He would not have been able to give us a hope for our future.
- In the world system today, Satan uses the hunger for power in us so that we 'dethrone' God in our lives and replace Him with instant power and glory, making us to be like gods (being short sighted, which we do not see), in order for us to not have revelation of God's plan for our lives, and therefore go astray.
- In Jesus we have destiny and He is the only One who can reveal that destiny to us (Eph 2:10). He knows the end from the beginning (Rev 1:8).
- Jesus restored our prophetic role (Gal 1:12; Eph 1:17).

Do you notice how finely entwined the priestly and prophetic dimensions are? We so need to realise that relationship and revelation go hand in hand; no relationship, no revelation and vice versa!

Satan was called the 'Guardian Cherub' or 'the Cherub who covers' before his fall (Eze 28:14&16), and he functioned in all three dimensions in the presence of God. His functioning in these dimensions was, however, limited and he desired more!

As he lost his position in God's presence (through his pride and rebellion) he also lost the ability to function in these dimensions. We, as people and the crown of God's creation (Isa 62:3), have now taken Satan's place and it is for this reason that he seeks to destroy mankind. It is the Lord's desire for us to grow in maturity and to function in the fullness of these dimensions, something that Satan could and will never have!

Summary:
In short, by combining chapter two and three, we can say that as we come together in the house of the Lord, the 'Tabernacle of David' is restored. In unity there is strength. Each person (nations, tribes, people) has authority (key/s) over something/some area in the spirit. By functioning in the dimensions that David functioned in (priest, prophet and king), we will be able to move into the fullness that God has planned for us as His representatives on this earth.

The order in which we move in these dimensions is: firstly the dimension of the PRIEST, then the dimension of the PROPHET and lastly only, the dimension of the KING. The reason for this will be explained in the following chapters.

APPLICATION STUDY GUIDE FOR CHAPTER THREE

1. Take time to allow the Holy Spirit to solidify these basic principles of priest, prophet and king in your mind and spirit by:
   a. Reading the chapter or parts of the chapter that you are uncertain about again.
   b. Studying the following scripture:
      - Heb 6:19 – 7:28
2. From the scripture above, are you able to identify the priestly, prophetic and kingly dimensions that Melchizedek functioned in?
3. In what area of your relationship with God has the enemy stolen from you?
4. Ask the Lord what He wants you to do to draw closer to Him.
5. In what area of revelation of Who the Lord is has the enemy stolen from you?
6. Ask the Holy Spirit to open up the Word of God in deeper dimensions to you as you spend time reading it.
7. In what area of your ability to rule has the enemy stolen from you?
8. Is there 'fear of man' in your life that keeps you from executing the Lord's instructions? Ask the Lord to break this cycle in your life.
   - The fear of man causes you to fear what man will think and say about you, as you are obedient to the Lord. This hinders you in walking with the Lord in complete freedom.

Pray with me:

"Father, I understand that the enemy is constantly seeking to destroy my priestly, prophetic and kingly role. Please sensitise my spirit to identify the lies that he wants to set in my heart so that I can resist him as I submit myself to you.

I recognise that you have a purpose for my life, and I now choose to follow You so that I may come to the fullness of living Your dream for my life. Lord I ask that You will strengthen me to do this. Amen."

CHAPTER FOUR

THE DIMENSION OF THE PRIEST

> "And I saw between the throne (with four living creatures) and the elders a Lamb standing, as if slain, having seven horns and seven eyes, which are the seven spirits of God, sent out into all the earth.
>
> When He had taken the book, the four living creatures and the twenty four elders fell down before the Lamb, each one holding a harp and golden bowls full of incense, which are the prayers of the saints."
>
> Rev 5:6&8

As we are positioned 'in Christ' we need to *firstly* operate in the dimension of being a priest! The dimension of a priest speaks of the relationship that we have with our Creator and heavenly Father.

It is only the priest who may minister to God (a king may not bring the sacrifice: 2 Chron 26:16-21) and therefore we approach the throne of God as a priest. In Rev 4:10 we read that the elders cast their crowns down before the Lord because there can be only one King when we enter His presence! Jesus, being the sacrificial Lamb of God (a lamb being the symbol of the priestly order), shows us that in order to come to the King we need to come in humility. To be in God's presence means to be face to Face with Him in His throne room (Holy of Holies in the tabernacle) where you draw close to Him to hear His heart beat. It is a place of intimacy; only you and God.

This priestly dimension is a heavenly dimension and therefore, as we draw into God's presence, He will give us **understanding**.

There are three phases of relationship, namely:
- Encounter with God; then
- Revelation of who He is; and total
- Surrender to Him and His destiny for your life.

How does this work?
- *Encounter with God* – You need to minister to God: You will only encounter God in fullness when you minister to Him and you do not come before Him for what He can give you. Worship is never about us but always about Him! Heb 13:15 says that we are to "continually offer up a sacrifice of praise..."
  If coming to the Lord had been to only receive from Him, why would praise then be a sacrifice?
- **Moses** continually remains in the Lord's presence and God speaks with Him deep and intimate things (Ex 19-34). Read Ex 33:18-23.

- Ex 33:20 "...for no man can see Me and live!"
  This statement does not speak of physical death, but of the fact that when we meet God, when we see Him face to Face, a part of our flesh dies and God brings a new deposit of Himself into our lives. Something supernatural happens when God meets with us and we embrace Him! Abraham met God face to Face and Isaac was born (Gen 18). Jacob saw God face to Face and his whole physical walk changed; there was peace with his enemies (Gen 32:24-32). Moses met God and carried His glory (Ex 34:1-3&29-35). Gideon encountered the Lord and brought freedom to Israel (Judges 6 and 7). Saul saw Jesus face to Face and his whole life perspective changed (Acts 9), and so we can continue to see how people's lives were affected when they come to the Lord to exult Him!
- Ex 33:21 "Behold, there is a place by Me, and you shall stand there on the rock."
  Ex 33:22 "...that I will put you in the cleft of the rock and cover you..."
  This place by (or with) God refers to our being able to hear His heart beat. It is His desire for us to be near Him, like John, who laid his head on the Master's chest (John 13:23-25). He could hear Jesus' heartbeat. Is it not interesting to note that of all the apostles in the New Testament it was John who received the revelation and wrote it down? Not even the apostle Paul, who moved in the supernatural dimensions that the Lord allowed him to walk in and wrote most of the New Testament, was chosen to write the book of Revelation. It was John, the beloved disciple! In the same way God wants us to be 'fine-tuned' to Him. It also speaks of a condition of body, mind and spirit. God caused Moses to stand on the rock (refuge/strength) so that he could have a firm foundation. Jesus is our firm foundation as He is the rock (Ps 27:5; Ps 40:2)! While the glory of the Lord was passing by, God caused Moses not just to stand on the rock but also to be in the rock (Ps 18:2; Ps 31:3). God wants to take us from just having Him as a foundation and experiencing Him, to a place of being in Him and knowing Him. The cleft speaks of a position in Christ; not just a mere standing on the Rock. Experiences pass us by, but our position in Him does not change. When God removed His hand, Moses was still in the rock. God is our covering; His hand of protection and guidance is always over us if we have found our position in Him. Too often we run from experience to experience because we are not positioned in Christ (John chapters 14, 15 and 16)!
- Ex 33:23 "...and you shall see My back..."
  Moses did not just see God's back[1], and it was not just the glory of God passing by either.

As God passed by He was giving Moses prophetic insight into things yet to come. For God it was in the past, a time hereafter (back), but for Moses it was in the future, or a time to come! One of the things that Moses saw was Christ's transfiguration on the mountain (Matt 17:1-9).

---

1 Strong's Concordance: H268, aw-khore', aw-khore', From H299; the *hinder* part; hence (adverbially) *behind, backward*; also (as facing north) the *West*. -after (-ward), back (part, -side, -ward), hereafter, (be-) hind (-er part), time to come, without.

- *Revelation of who He is – Our disability is perfected in His ability.* Read Rev 5:1-5 again. John was devastated that there was no one seen to be worthy, and he realised his own shortcomings. However, hope flared again when one of the elders told him to look to Christ! Jesus is the only worthy One. As you discover His true identity, you can receive freedom in finding yourself in Him. As your eyes turn to Him, you will discover who He is and then you discover who you are in Him. All your lack and disability is taken away because He IS able. Our life starts at the throne of grace, not the cross.
- **Samuel** ministered before the Lord no matter what was taking place in the temple (1 Sam 1:24-28; 1 Sam 2:11, 18-21; 1 Sam 3:1-21; 1 Sam 7:17). When we read these passages we see that in spite of so much disability, disorder, chaos and sin in the temple, Samuel kept his focus on God and his relationship with Him.
  - Remember that the object of your affection (or attention) is also the object of your worship. If your focus is on your circumstances you can end up 'worshiping' them instead of God. You may not be distracted in your relationship with God, no matter what is happening around you, so that you may grow in stature! The more focused you are in your relationship with God the more He will raise you up and draw you into His presence.
  - We read in 1 Sam 4:4 how Hophni and Phinehas, the sons of Eli, took the Ark of the Covenant out to the battlefield because they thought it would bring them the victory. By this time God was no longer with them. The Ark was not in the temple and yet Samuel fellowshipped with God. We need to understand that God will not be limited to a 'box', and this is what we do when we limit Him in our thinking!
  - We are to impart to others what we receive from the Lord. You can only impart (to bestow a part of; to give; to communicate; to make known) to people if you have been in God's presence to receive. What you have not received cannot be imparted, and therefore the more you remain in God's presence the more you are able to impart. Impartation means that I am taking of what I have and placing it in you, not on you. You can also not impart what is not yours to impart! Further, you need to ensure that the people you are imparting to will take responsibility for what they are given. For example: you, who have been baptised in the Holy Spirit, have the gifts of the Spirit imparted by the Spirit Himself. It is now your responsibility to stir the gifts and function in them! When you pray for someone to be filled with the Holy Spirit you cannot impart the gifts of the Spirit because they are His alone to impart; you can only pray for the release of these gifts.

[2]Samuel's anointing was imparted to two people, namely Saul (1 Sam 10:1) and David (1 Sam 16:13), but only one received the fullness of it and functioned in that fullness. Saul was anointed with a flask of oil (representing man's choice) but it never affected his character. David, on the other hand, was anointed with a horn of oil (representing God's choice) and he moved into that fullness.

---

[2] Reference in this paragraph is made to the book "Apostolic Strategies Affecting Nations" by Dr. Jonathan David.

Even though David made mistakes, he allowed God to shape and mould his character to such a degree that he was called 'a man after God's own heart' (Acts 13:22). The significance of the horn being used as a vessel to contain the oil lies in the fact that an animal had to die in order to obtain the horn. This speaks of sacrifice and dying to self. Anointing is imparted but together with anointing comes the responsibility to steward it.

- *Surrender – You can only rule as a king once you have been a priest!* You cannot understand the Kingdom and how it functions if you do not know the King. This talks about a love relationship and being with Him. You get to know how the Kingdom functions because you are at the side of the King as He rules His kingdom. Jesus knew how the Kingdom functioned because He was in constant communication with the Father (John 5:19).
- **Paul** saw Christ in the glorified dimension. He never knew the man Jesus like the other disciples, but after Christ revealed himself to Paul on the road to Damascus, he saw things in the same dimension in which Christ was revealed to him (Acts 9:3-6). It is for this reason that Paul had the ability to teach with the revelation he taught in. Let us take a look at Acts 9:1-19 to see how we can affect the area around us. Remember that influence comes from relationship.
    - Acts 9:5 (read from verse 3) "And he said, 'Who are You, Lord?' and He said, 'I am Jesus whom you are persecuting.'"
    You need to internalise the principles of God. Often we know the principles, and we speak about them, but what we don't have is revelation of them. Revelation only comes when we ask 'who are you Lord' and we receive the answer in our spirit. We gain revelation by listening to the Voice of God.
    - Acts 9:6 "but get up and enter the city, it will be told you what you must do."
    Firstly we need to heed to the *immediate instructions* that the Lord gives us, and by doing so He will bring us to a position where we can receive detailed instructions of what He wants us to do. Often we miss the first instructions that God gives us, and because of that we never get to the fullness of what He wants to give to us. The 'city' speaks of a place of refuge. God will place you in a place of protection so that you have clarity when He speaks to you.
    - Acts 9:20 "and immediately he began to proclaim Jesus in the synagogues, saying, 'He is the Son of God.'"
    God will take what you wanted for your own gain and turn it for His glory. Many times we have our own intentions as to why we do things (Paul's was to persecute the Christians), but God will work in our hearts so that His intentions are impressed onto our hearts. We must always go into a situation (or place) with the intention to penetrate and bring change, not just to make an impact! An impact is short lived but penetration breaks into a situation and brings the change from the inside. The best way to explain this is when an army attacks a city to gain possession; the aim is never to just surround it and bang against the wall bringing fear to its inhabitants. Rather, it is to penetrate it so that a take-over can be established. This was Paul's success; everything he did, he did in order to penetrate.

- Acts 9:7 "...hearing the voice but seeing no one."
  Acts 9:8 "...and leading him by the hand, they brought him to Damascus."
  Those around you *will not necessarily have the complete picture* of what is happening to you, but they will be *faithful to lead you* to the place where you will be *repositioned* to hear the detailed instructions from God. Every person needs a few friends who are close to him or her, who will be of help at the right time and as the Lord directs. It is important to be sensitive in your spirit about who you allow close to you, because the enemy will use any chance to mislead you by placing the wrong people beside you. Not everyone you know needs to know the detail of everything in your life. Jesus had many followers, but He had only twelve disciples, of whom three were chosen to witness His transfiguration (Matt 17:1-9). Only one of these three was allowed to place his head on Jesus' chest (John 13:23-25; John 21:20).
- Acts 9:9 "...and neither ate nor drank"
  We need *to live a fasted life* (Isa 58). What does this mean? Very simply it means that we need to come to a place where we are in total surrender to Him, allowing the Lord to work in our lives freely; a place of living out Kingdom principles. It happens so often that we call before the Lord in repentance, but afterward continue to compromise in what He has said.
- Acts 9:12 "and he has seen in a vision a man named Ananias ..."
  God will show you *the people you are to work with* closely and from whom you are to receive instruction and guidance. It is important for us to realise that we are part of a body and that we need to function as a body. No one body part can function on its own and apart from the body (1 Cor 12:12-27). Therefore, God places people along side of us who firstly disciple us and teach us what we need to know, and secondly help us in what we are called by Him to do. The time for 'lone rangers' has come to an end and the time for team work has begun.
- Acts 9:15 "...For he is a chosen instrument of Mine, ..."
  Realise and accept that you are a chosen instrument in God's hand. Do you believe the dreams God has about you and that He is able to bring you to the fullness there of? Never say, "Is there anyone else Lord?" because by doing this, you are denying the destiny God has purposed for your life and cutting off His grace to move in that destiny.
  - Acts 9:13&14 "But Ananias answered, 'Lord, I have heard from many about this man, how much harm he did to Your saints ..."
    Please note that if you are the one God has called to use to impart into someone else's life, do not argue with God but be obedient in the matter. We do not always see what God sees, and may even be influenced by what we hear from others, just like Ananias. It is for this reason that we need God's perspective on the matter.
- Acts 9:16 "for I will show him how much he must suffer for My name's sake."
  With the call of God upon your life, *grace is released to complete the work* He has called you to do. No matter what your destiny is, together with that destiny God releases the ability and internal dynamics to fulfil it to the last detail. We need to look at the word 'suffer' and receive revelation from the

- Lord to see the 'grace' in it.
- Acts 9:18 (read from verse 17) "…there fell from his eyes something like scales, … and he got up and was baptised;"
  Understand that the *Holy Spirit is the One who empowers* you to complete the course. You cannot function out of your own strength and you need to be dependent on the Spirit. Many times God will place 'scales' on our eyes so that we are forced to see in the spirit and not look at the situation with our natural eyes. These scales often come in the form of circumstances and tests that cross our path, and are divine interventions in our lives from God, not from the enemy!
- Acts 9:19 "and he took food and was strengthened."
  Receive the spiritual food that is given to you from the correct Source and it will strengthen you. Paul spent seven years tapping into God and drawing from Him. If your source is polluted, your life will be also. What you 'eat' is what you are.

The more you grow in your relationship with the Lord, the more you will function in the fullness of this priestly dimension. As you come to a certain fullness of maturity you will start breaking through to the next dimension, which is the dimension of the prophetic.

APPLICATION STUDY GUIDE FOR CHAPTER FOUR

1. Do you fully understand the dimension of the priest? Take time to allow the Holy Spirit to solidify these principles in your mind and spirit by:
   a. Reading the chapter or parts of the chapter that you are uncertain about again.
   b. Studying the following scriptures:
      - Heb 4:14-16
      - Heb 5:1-6
      - Heb 8:7-13
2. How can functioning in the priestly dimension help you in your daily walk with God concerning your destiny? Take some time to write down what it is that God wants to do in and through your life.
3. Worship is one of the easiest and effective ways to stir your spirit man to focus on the Lord. Set aside time to honour God for who He is in your life. Choose songs that speak about who He is and not necessarily what He does. Do this regularly and do not let time limit you! Set aside enough time.

Pray with me:

"Lord, I ask that You will forgive me where I came into Your presence demanding from You, and disrespecting You. Lord Jesus, teach me to take up my priestly role and be a living sacrifice of praise in Your sight.

Give me understanding, Lord, that I may know who You are. May my words, thoughts and actions be pleasing to You always as I minister to You, and may I always be in Your presence. Amen."

CHAPTER FIVE

THE DIMENSION OF THE PROPHET

> "And they sang a new song, saying,
> 'Worthy are You to take the book and to break its seals;
> for You were slain, and purchased for God with Your blood
> men from every tribe and tongue and people and nation."
>
> Rev 5:9

As we are positioned 'in Christ' we need to *secondly* operate in the dimension of being a prophet! The dimension of a prophet speaks of the revelations that we receive when we are in the presence of our Lord. Please note that this dimension of being a 'prophet' does NOT refer to *the five-fold ministry function of a prophet* (Eph 4:11) *or to the gift of prophecy* that is given by the Holy Spirit (1 Cor 12:4-11)!

The word 'prophecy' simply refers to the ability to see, identify and discern what the Lord is showing you in the heavens and cannot be used as an argument to prophecy or to function in the five-fold ministry of a prophet. The ministry function of a prophet is only for some who are chosen and called by the Lord for the purpose of equipping the saints and bringing the body of Christ into maturity (Eph 4:12&13). The gift of prophecy is available for all to function in, but you must be baptised with the Holy Spirit; you must desire the gift, you must stir the gift and practise it. However, although functioning in the dimension of a prophet is for all sons and daughters of God, it is linked to and parallels your priestly function! The deeper your relationship with God, the more He will reveal to you! It cannot and will not function in any other way.

Functioning in the dimension of a prophet allows us to have **knowledge** to break open the depths of the Lord and His Word; it is *not* connected to foretelling the future!

There are three phases of revelation, namely:
- Identify the voice of the Lord and then see and hear what the Lord is speaking.
- Identify and discern if what you see / hear is to be declared.
- Bring forth the revelation into the earth realm by speaking what is revealed so that it can be built into the spirit atmosphere.

How does this work?
- *Identify, see and hear – You need the ability to see and hear in the spirit:* If you miss the ability to see in the spirit you will not be able to establish God's Kingdom on earth, for which the sons of God have been called (Rom 8:16-

23). This prophetic dimension enables you to see what the Lord is doing in the heavens so that you can emulate it on earth (Matt 6:10). We see God's precepts, principles and Kingdom rule.

- **Samuel** was a seer (1 Sam 9:9, 18&19) and what he saw in the presence of God he spoke out. Although he was functioning in the five-fold ministry of a prophet, I would like to use his example because of his relationship with God.
  - Samuel firstly had to learn to identify the voice of the Lord before he could commune with God (1 Sam 3:1-14). As a little boy Samuel had not been able to recognise the voice of the Lord, although he had been 'ministering before the Lord' (1 Sam 2:11&18) because "word from the Lord was rare in those days; visions were infrequent." 1 Sam 3:1

    Once Samuel knew the voice of the Lord, he was able to shut out all other voices and he grew steadily in his relationship with God (1 Sam 3:21). No matter what happened around Samuel in the temple, he just kept his focus on the Lord! We need to do the same: shut out what is not from God and keep our focus on Him! The enemy so often causes us to focus on our circumstances and we need to make a choice, like Samuel did, to keep our eyes on our Creator!
  - Samuel spoke one hundred percent of God's Word, one hundred percent of the time. There was no compromise and nothing of himself! We need to emulate only what we see God doing and what we hear Him saying because then only will we be entrusted to see more! None of our own opinions and interpretations can be added or mixed into what God says.
  - Every word that Samuel spoke came into being (1 Sam 3:19-21) but it came from having a relationship with God, which was the platform for opening up the spirit dimension. Everyone knew what Samuel said was true because the Lord confirmed it.

- *Identify and discern* – Is that which is revealed to you in the spirit relevant to the situation at hand: What you experience in worship must be shared with wisdom! Not everything you see is necessarily for you or other people specifically.
- **John**, the 'loved' disciple of Jesus, wrote the book 'Revelation'. To him was revealed many awesome things which he penned down! However, there were also things that he saw where God instructed him not to write down what was spoken, although it was revealed to Him (Rev 10:3&4).

There are many things that we can see and hear when we travel in a vehicle from point 'A' to point 'B', but not everything that we see or hear is of importance for our journey. We may see houses, trees, animals, road signs and other vehicles, but only the road signs, the route we follow, and the other traffic is of importance to us.

The same applies in the spirit. Just because the Lord reveals something to you does not mean that it is for others to know. It is crucial that we discern what needs to be revealed and what needs to stay between you and the Lord.

This discernment brings accuracy, without which you cannot hit the mark.

- *Bring forth the revelation into the earth realm by speaking what is revealed so that it can be built into the spirit atmosphere:* What is revealed to you needs to be declared / spoken into circumstances and people's lives until it manifests. There are three specific areas that we should speak clearly in, as we see in the heavens.
- **Elijah** (1 Kings 17 – 2 Kings 2) spoke in all three of these areas:
  o *Sin and idolatry*: He addressed sin clearly and did not compromise on what he spoke concerning sin. He confronted everyone who opposed God and he exposed idolatry (1 Kings 18:18-40). When we have been in God's presence we will clearly see sin and idolatry for what it is, and we will be able to speak against it and see God bring it to the fall in people's lives. The question is whether we speak clearly enough regarding this point, or are we also compromising? Remember to speak with God's love toward the person and with hate toward the sin he/she commits.
  o *Circumstances verses Truth*: Elijah spoke into the atmosphere and the climate changed. There was no rain for three years after Elijah made the declaration, and only after he prayed did it rain again (1 Kings 17:1; 1 Kings 18:41-45). When we speak into the 'atmosphere' of our circumstances we can change the spiritual climate around us; but, we can only know what the change should be if we have been in God's presence because that is where we see/hear what to speak. It is important that we always speak truth (what is God saying about the matter) and not the circumstance (what the enemy wants us to believe is unchangeable/truth). This does not just concern our own circumstances but also the circumstances of our fellow believers. We need to 'build' into the spirit! When we speak God's truth, we build, but when we speak our circumstances we will see the negative manifest.
  o *Impartation*: Elijah prepared the next generation by building into Elisha's life and raising him up as the next prophet (1 Kings 19:19-21; 2 Kings 2:1-14). God wants to use your 'voice' to 'impart' or 'implant' revelation into other people's lives so that they can grow and mature in their relationship with God. What revelations do you implant into the next spiritual generation, and is your voice clear enough so that they will follow the Lord? Discipleship is crucial for this day and age.

- Another person who declared into the spirit realm and saw the manifestations thereof is **Paul**. Although Paul functioned from an apostolic viewpoint, he still used the basic principles that we need to use when we function in this dimension of 'prophetic' order. Let us look at 1 Cor 2:1-10 to learn these important principles concerning 'speaking revelation'.
  o I Cor 2:1 "... I did not come with superiority of speech or of wisdom ..."
    Paul spoke nothing out of his own wisdom or understanding, but only what God had revealed to him. There was no eloquence of tongues or 'learned' wisdom that aided him in his speaking. Just like Paul did not lean on his own understanding (Prov 3:5) but on that of Christ, we need to move our

desires and ideas out of the way and rely only on the Spirit of God and what He reveals.

- I Cor 2:2 "For I determined to know nothing among you except Jesus Christ, and Him crucified."

This speaks of a specific dimension of revelation that Paul had, namely Christ and our identity in Him, and what He did. Note that some revelation is for *all* people (babies in the spirit) but all revelation is for some people (those who are mature fathers in the spirit). Once again: revelation is simultaneous to the level of maturity that you have in Christ; the more you mature the more is revealed to you.

- I Cor 2:3&4 "…and my message and my preaching were not in persuasive words of wisdom, but in demonstration of the Spirit and of power,"

If you have the revelation from the Spirit of God then the power is released! It is not what you know but whom you know, because revelation will always flow from the source that you are connected to. In Zech 4:6 it says that we are not to do things out of might or power, this being carnal power, but should allow the Holy Spirit to move. Please remember that when the Spirit of the Lord is doing a work, no matter how gentle, He will always move in power.

- I Cor 2:5 "so that your faith would not rest on the wisdom of man, but on the power of God."

Faith in God is based not on wisdom from man that is made up of own opinions and wrong doctrines, but on the revelation knowledge given by the Holy Spirit and the Word, and the power that is released by it as you live it. Remember that revelation on its own will not bring the breakthrough; revelation must be applied. Building comes by doing/living.

- I Cor 2:6 "Yet we do speak wisdom among those who are mature; a wisdom, however, not of this age nor of the rulers of this age, who are passing away."

It is important for you to come to a certain level of maturity to be able to receive the revelation contained in that dimension or higher level. 'Of this age' denotes the current 'times', or chronology of time we live in, whereas 'age' in general refers to segments of time. 'Rulers of this age' makes reference to the people in position of worldly authority, but also to the spiritual forces of evil that these people receive their revelations and power from. The wisdom that Paul speaks of is obtained from God only, and cannot be compared to the wisdom by which these earthly rulers exercise rule, and to the source from which they draw, which is a temporal thing as they are 'passing away'.

- I Cor 2:7 "…speak God's wisdom in a mystery, the hidden wisdom which God predestined …"

I Cor 2:8 "the wisdom which none of the rulers of this age has understood;" 'In a mystery' makes reference to the revelation of Christ's death and resurrection and the fullness pertaining to it; not merely salvation, but the fullness of life that God intended for you that is made available to you through Christ Jesus (John 10:10; Eph 3:19). The closer you draw to Him the more understanding you will receive of this specific mystery. 'Predestined' speaks of the destiny that has been laid out for your life by the Lord. As you move closer to God you will also be able to declare more and more of your destiny into the spirit world. How awesome it is to move in faith when you know where the Lord is leading your life! The rulers of this age are blinded and cannot see what you see. This is why when you start speaking things of the spirit, people will often not understand. Do not be discouraged by this; instead be encouraged that you can see what others cannot see, and that you may be an instrument in the Lord's hand. It is for this reason that you need to discern what you speak in public and what needs to be kept private. Too often people make the mistake of proclaiming publicly what should have been kept in the heart, and suffer unnecessary criticism and judgement, even from fellow Christians.

- I Cor 2:9 "...Things which eye has not seen and ear not heard, and which have not entered the heart of man, all that God has prepared for those who love Him."
God is waiting for you and me to draw on and receive revelation of things that have always been, but have not been revealed to us yet. These dimensions are both natural (eye and ear) and supernatural (heart). 'God has prepared' everything for us; all we need to do is to be willing to take hold of all that the Lord wants to release. The only prerequisite is a pure heart and clean hands. To such people God will not just reveal, but He will also allow them to walk in the revelations. This is clearly expressed in the word 'love' which speaks of relationship with our Lord. Please take note that there are some mysteries that can only be accessed by the apostolic grace (Eph 4:11-13), but all mystery pertaining to personal destiny (His dream for your life) and growth is available to us (Eph 1:17&18). The apostolic grace breaks open for the people, and the people live in that which is broken open with further revelation from the Holy Spirit. This principle can easily be explained by making the following illustration: A house owner who has the keys to a house can unlock and open the door to that house. This allows you to enter into and explore the different rooms in it. Prior to the door being unlocked and opened you can only see into the rooms from the outside, but they are not accessible to you.
- I Cor 2:10 "...for the Spirit searches all things"
It is the Spirit of God who reveals to us all the mysteries (1 Cor 2:11-13).

The Spirit searches everything, including man's heart, and brings truth into our lives. In John 14:26 two aspects are revealed:
- Firstly, He 'teaches you all things' concerning the depths of God. There are so many different dimensions of God, and because the Spirit also searches the depths of God, He is the one who will bring you insight to Who the Lord is.
- The Holy Spirit will also 'remind you of all' that Jesus taught through the word. That which is taught will also be available when you need it!

I trust that you have grasped the importance of the need to continue to grow in your priestly function (relationship with God) no matter how well you are functioning in the prophetic dimension. As you now continue to draw into God's presence and not just function but live in the priestly dimension, you will start breaking out into the kingly dimension on the earth.

APPLICATION STUDY GUIDE FOR CHAPTER FIVE

1. Do you fully understand the dimension of the prophet? Take some time to allow the Holy Spirit to solidify these principles in your mind and spirit by:
   a. Reading the chapter or parts of the chapter that you are uncertain about again.
   b. Studying the following scriptures:
      - Heb 4:12&13
      - Rom 11:33-36
      - Matt 6:33
2. How can functioning in godly revelation help you in your daily walk with God? Take time to write down what it is that God wants to do:
   a. In your life: It may be further healing, building of principles, purifying, etc. Act on what the Lord shows you.
   b. Through your life: Remember that God can use you right there in your job or family; you don't need to become a pastor or missionary to be used by the Lord, unless He calls you to do that!
3. Now ask the Lord for scripture to confirm the above. Write these down. You may already have word that the Lord has given you. Write this down and ask God if there is another level that He wants to reveal to you.
4. Declare what you have seen in the spirit concerning your life through constant prayer, and build it into the spirit until you see the manifestation thereof.
5. Reading the Word of God is of utmost importance for the renewing of your mind, but it is the deeper revelation from the Holy Spirit of the word, which will help you to make those positive shifts in your life. Set aside time to study the scriptures. Ask the Lord which book in the Bible you need to start reading. Ensure that you have enough time, and do not just read chapter by chapter but read as the Spirit leads, meditating on the word (Ps 1:2).

Pray with me:

"Lord I call to You and ask that You will give me knowledge and show me great and unsearchable things that I have not known or understood. I pray too that I will not just have the revelation, but that I will live by that revelation, and have the ability to share with others so that they too can live as I do.

Lord I also ask that you will enlarge the capacity of my spirit man to be able to contain what You reveal to me so that it will not be lost, and so that it may come to maturity.

I praise You Lord that I may be in a position where You reveal Your heart to me. Amen."

CHAPTER SIX

THE DIMENSION OF THE KING

"And one of the elders said to me, 'Stop weeping; behold, the Lion that is from the tribe of Judah, the Root of David, has overcome so as to open the book and its seven seals.'

And every created thing which is in heaven and on the earth
and under the earth and on the sea, and all things in them, I heard saying,
'To Him who sits on the throne, and unto the Lamb, be blessing and honour and
glory and dominion forever and ever.'"

Rev 5:5&13

As we are positioned 'in Christ' we need to *finally* operate in the dimension of being a king! If we read Rev 5:5 the elder says that the Lion of the tribe of Judah has prevailed, but when John looks up, he sees a Lamb as if slain (Rev 5:6). This clearly shows us that all flows out of the priestly dimension and victory comes from life in Christ!

Functioning in the dimension of a king is for all God's sons, and it is the way in which you express the Lord's dominion that He has given you on the earth. But, it is once again linked to and parallel to your priestly function! The deeper your relationship with God, the more authority and power will be released to you and a larger area of influence will be entrusted to you. Through the kingly dimension, you come to express your relationship with God and what you have seen/heard from the Lord.

Being in an earthly dimension, God gives us **wisdom** as to how to rule and function in this kingly role.

There are three phases of rulership, namely:
- Receive **understanding** (from the priestly / heavenly dimension) of God's government and rule; then
- Internalise these principles and live by them, so that you can
- Establish the Kingdom of God wherever you go using God given **wisdom**.

How does this work?
- *Receive understanding of God's government and rule – because of what you see and proclaim, His kingdom is firstly established in your own heart:* If you do not see the Kingdom established in your spirit you will not see it established around you.
- Not much is said about **Enoch** in the scriptures, but what we do know is that he was righteous before the Lord (Gen 5:19-24; Heb 11:5). His genealogy is recorded in 1 Chron 1:3 and Luke 3:37&38.
- Although scripture says in Jude 1:14&15 that he prophesied, he was still

functioning in the kingly dimension. We can see this in the content of his 'prophecy', in these verses, where he speaks of the lack of righteousness and God coming to execute judgement and convict all the ungodly people because of their ungodly deeds. One of the most powerful ways to 'execute judgement' is simply by living in Kingdom righteousness wherever you go! In 1 Thess 2:10-13 it declares that God calls us into His Kingdom, and His word performs a work in us so as to establish that Kingdom in our hearts.

- Enoch walked with God, and this means to do justice, to love kindness and to walk humbly WITH God according to Mic 6:8. All you do, you do with God and not for Him. Sons work with God in His Kingdom (we are co-heirs with Christ) and servants work for Him (they work for remuneration). You are no longer a sinner, but you are a son of God! In the Old Testament people were 'saints' of God, whereas in the New Testament we are 'sons' of God because of what Christ did in reconciling us with the Father.

- *Internalise these principles and live by them – take control of situations:* As the Government of God's Kingdom is established in your heart, you can now start to take charge of your negative circumstances.

- **Samuel** moved in such a governmental authority that as long as he was the ruler over Israel, the enemies could not enter the land (1 Sam 7:5-13), and all the land that was taken by the Philistines was regained (1 Sam 7:14). We need to carry the government of God in our lives, so that wherever we go, we can establish His Kingdom. Government is not just authority, but also principles and dimensions, and the ability to live in them and exercise them. You are a kingdom carrier before you can establish the Kingdom (2 Cor 5:19-21). As an ambassador you first need to learn all there is to know about the laws and protocols of the nation you represent before you are sent to another country as a representative.

- [1] Samuel's anointing could also be placed on a group of people for a period of time (1 Sam 19:20-24). The mantle of Samuel's anointing subdued the power of the murderous spirit in Saul. It exposed the power of satanic activity in Saul and it quickened the gifts within Saul. It also enlarged his spirit to contain more of God. This means that as you learn to carry the government of God, you will start having victory over the lies of the enemy and over spiritual attacks in your life; people's motives will become clear to you and they will be affected by the Holy Spirit when close to you; finally, people's spirit capacity will be enlarged to contain more of God as they move under your anointing!

    However, it is their choice to allow God to change their lives. Saul resisted this change and the end result was very clear (1 Sam 31:4-6).

- When Saul stripped naked before Samuel (1 Sam 19:24) he was showing his vulnerability and emptiness. Your enemies will stand naked before you showing their vulnerability to you. The Lord now starts to rule over your enemies.

---

1   Reference in this paragraph is made to the book "Apostolic Strategies Affecting Nations" by Dr. Jonathan David.

- *Establish the Kingdom of God wherever you go – all that was made available to you when you were in His presence you need to manifest on the earth:* Once the Kingdom principles are established in your life, and you can take charge of what affects you (you have learned to activate your will and rule in circumstances), you are ready to rule wherever you go and be a vessel through which God establishes His Kingdom on the earth.

  Jesus was the Father's house on earth (John 14:2 – Refer to page 17 in this book) and He showed His disciples what He carried within Him on the mount of transfiguration (Matt 7:1-9), but we also need to understand that He was not merely showing them that He was carrying the Kingdom, but showing them how to carry the Kingdom and its dimensions!

  You must realise that God wants you to be a Kingdom carrier! In 1 Corinthians 6:19 it says that our body is a temple of the Holy Spirit and in Ephesians 3:19 we read "… that you may be filled up to *ALL* the fullness of God." (Emphasis mine).

  The NIV bible says "…that you may be filled to the measure of all the fullness of God."

  This body of ours is the temple of the Holy Spirit and it houses all things of the Kingdom through Him!

  You can carry all that heaven has sent (Kingdom of God, truth, dimensions of the Holy Spirit, the will of the Father, the power, the life, etc), or 'the measure of' in your body. The amount of Kingdom you carry depends on your relationship with God and your maturity in Christ. **The more you mature, the more of heaven you can carry within.** Remember that Kingdom is not something that is carried on the outside, but is something that is carried on the inside and flows to the outside. Kingdom must flow OUT! We don't need to build an external tabernacle to 'house' the Lord because we are now His tabernacle! This means that where ever we go, the Kingdom of God must start to break out because it flows from us.

  I believe that, for example, we have focussed too much on getting the demonic out, and have forgotten to bring the Kingdom in. For when the Kingdom of Heaven comes in, the demonic automatically must go out! It is a matter of perspective change.

- **Paul** was able to "download" governmental dimensions from God and manifest them through those who were with him (Acts 19:9-41). Everywhere he went, the Kingdom of God manifested and evil was exposed on earth as it is in heaven (Matt 6:10). Paul affected every area of society.

- Through Paul and his disciples the Lord did great healings (Acts 19:11&12). The 'handkerchiefs' and 'aprons' spoken of in verse twelve were not pieces of cloth that Paul laid his hands on, prayed over, and then had people carry them to the sick! He was a tent maker by 'profession' and these were his sweat bands and aprons that he used while he was working. The glory of God was so present in Paul that it saturated even his clothing. When his disciples took these to the ill, they were healed. We can see the same situation with Jesus and the woman with the issue of blood. The glory of God so saturated Jesus' garments that when she touched the hem of His cloak, she was healed (Matt 9:20&21; Mark 5:25-29; Luke 8:44). We can never imitate the power of God.

- See what happened to the sons of a priest who had no relationship with Christ when they tried to command demons in Acts 19:14-17. The Lord wants to use us as instruments of healing and grace.
- Paul affected the area of false religion and occult. Just through his rulership and God's presence that he carried, God caused the evil to be exposed and people to be set free from these practices (Acts 19:18-20). The principle of 'Kingdom in and demons out' is very clearly illustrated here. Please note that I do not mean to say that we are never to address demons and resist them, but we need to flow with the Holy Spirit in this matter, and our 'work' will surely be easier if the Kingdom of Heaven is manifested! We are to set people free from demonic oppression by bringing it to the light and truth of God.
- Paul even caused a stirring and reformation in the business world (Acts 19:22-41) and met government leaders (Acts 25:23; Acts 26:28). Throughout all this he ministered and shared about the Kingdom of God. There is no area where we cannot exercise our kingly authority on this earth as long as we remain sensitive to the Holy Spirit and, like Jesus, do only what we see the Father do (John 5:19).

When we rule as kings – A lesson from David's life

Take a few minutes to read 2 Sam 7:8-17 so that you can follow the next few points.

- 2 Sam 7:8 "… to be a ruler over my people."
  God makes us rulers over His people. This in effect means that we are to bring love and hope to those who have lost hope. We are to guide and instruct so that people may take their place in His Kingdom. We are also to protect the weak so that they may grow strong in the Lord.
- 2 Sam 7:9 "I have been with you wherever you have gone and have cut off all your enemies; and I will make you a great name…"
  It is so awesome to see that as we follow this road, God is with us and He removes all our enemies. Just as Satan left Jesus until an 'opportune' time (Luke 4:13), so God will bring us to a place of victory! 'Great name' symbolises that God will increase your area of influence, just as the name of a well-known ruler or person increases their influence.
- 2 Sam 7:10 "I will also appoint a place for my people Israel and will plant them, … nor will the wicked afflict them any more"
  God will establish you in a position of rulership in Him and you will not be moved or removed. As our standing in the Lord is secure, our foundations are sure, and there will be no more afflictions. All too often we suffer afflictions because we do not exercise our rule in the circumstances presented to us, and all too often we cannot rule because we are not standing on a firm foundation. Remember that 'afflictions' come because of circumstances, and 'enemies' are those who wage war against you. God will bring victory on both fronts!
- 2 Sam 7:11 "… I will give you rest from all your enemies. … The Lord will make a house for you."
  Your enemies will not come against you because the Lord will start to fight

these battles for you and subdue those who rise up against you (1 Sam 17:47; Ps 24:8; Zech 14:3). There will come a turning point in your life, where the battle truly 'belongs to the Lord'; because this is a heritage that we have from God, He will vindicate us (Isa 54:17)! God will give you a place from which you will be established (household / family / disciples), and it will steadily increase, for He is a God of increase. The Lord's desire is to establish[2] His Kingdom and rule, and because you are part of His plan He will also establish you!

- 2 Sam 7:12 "When your days are complete… I will rise up your descendant after you, who will come forth from you, and I will establish his kingdom."

God will raise up people after you who will carry the same vision, dimensions and dynamics that you have, and He will establish their rule. These 'descendants' are not necessarily 'blood' descendants, but can also be 'descendants' in the 'spirit'; those whom you have imparted your life to, and raised in the spirit as sons. It is God Who establishes their kingdom rule, and therefore there is an enlarging of what He has placed in you even after you have passed away; a continuation of your legacy through your offspring (physical or spiritual), which is founded by God.

- 2 Sam 7:13 "He shall build a house for My name, and I will establish the throne of his kingdom forever."

Your offspring will build a place of worship for the Lord (move into a dimension of relationship) that you have not had, but because you have laid the foundations in their lives, God releases a new level. God's rule will be established permanently through you and your descendants.

- 2 Sam 7:14&15 "I will be a father to him and he will be a son to Me … but My lovingkindness shall not depart from him …"

God will adopt your descendants, discipline them when they do wrong, and love them as He has loved you. There will be grace upon them to walk in righteousness, for He is a God of righteousness.

- 2 Sam 7:16 "Your house and your kingdom shall endure before Me forever; your throne shall be established forever."

God will use the dimensions of rule and dominion that have been established by Him, through you, so that others can have access to it and function in it. We need to realise that God is a God of the generations, which can be seen throughout this passage, and that is why He does not only use us, but also our generations to come to establish His Kingdom and Kingdom work on the earth. So often we only think of the 'now generation', but forget to impart into the next so that there can be a continual building. For too long each new generation needed to start from 'scratch', but God is now taking us into a time when we need to see the importance of the generations beyond us; those not even born, for He has a destiny for them!

---

[2] Webster's dictionary: to settle or fix firmly in a position; a place in possession or in power; to found.

I believe that if we, as children of God, learn to function in the fullness of the kingly dimension, we will see His power released and manifested through us in awesome ways, for this is the Lord's desire! Always remember though, that relationship with the Creator is the vessel that carries the Creator's power. We have power and authority:

- To cast out demons and heal the sick: Matt 10:1; Mark 3:15; Luke 9:1
- To rule in the market place: Luke 19:17&19; Acts 19:23-41
- To make disciples, baptise and teach the word: Matt 28:18-20; Mark 3:14; Mark 16:15
- Over all the power of the enemy: Luke 10:19&20
- To be God's witnesses wherever we go: Acts 1:8

These are all areas that we need to exercise rulership in! As you start to rule, you will also notice that you will become more effective in your everyday life as a child of God because you will learn to take authority over circumstances and move in victory.

APPLICATION STUDY GUIDE FOR CHAPTER SIX

1. Do you fully understand the dimension of the king? Take time to allow the Holy Spirit to solidify these principles in your mind and spirit by:
    a. Reading the chapter or parts of the chapter that you are uncertain about again.
    b. Studying the following scriptures:
        - 1 Cor 4:20
        - Matt 4:17
        - Col 1:13-20
        - 2 Thess 2:12&13
2. How can functioning in the kingly dimension help you in your daily walk with God? What are the areas that you need to gain breakthrough in, and how are you going to do it?
3. Do you understand the difference between the gospel of salvation, which is often spoken about by man, and the gospel of the Kingdom (of God), which Jesus speaks about (Matt 4:23; Acts 19:8)? List the differences. What does the Lord want us to proclaim and live?
4. Hear from the Lord how you are to start ruling in the following areas:
    a. Home / family
    b. Work
    c. Social / friends

Pray with me:

"Lord, forgive me for not expressing Your rule on earth through my life. I have been too focussed on myself, and have not obeyed Your command to 'have dominion'. I declare that You have created me to rule there where You have placed me, and that I am able to do so by the power of Your Holy Spirit.

Lord, give me boldness to stand for You, and wisdom to establish Your Kingdom wherever You lead me. Amen."

CHAPTER SEVEN

UNDERSTANDING AND FUNCTIONING IN THE TIMES OF GOD

We have now come to the place where we need to *function* in the *dimensions* of the key of David and *use* the Keys of the Kingdom of heaven.

The way this works is as follows: The key of David is the ability to function firstly in the priestly dimension, thereafter the prophetic (perceiving) dimension and then expressing all that has been revealed to us through the kingly dimension. Further, it speaks of the authority that is released to us to open what no one can shut, and to shut what no one can open *in the spirit world.*

Once we have an open door (in a specific area), we can use the keys of the Kingdom of Heaven to bind and loose things *on the earth*, following the decrees that have been declared by the Lord (Matt 6:10), through that open door in the spirit. Remember that you see and hear the decree as you function in the priestly and prophetic dimensions. You have the authority and power to address things on earth as you function in the kingly dimension. The keys of the Kingdom of Heaven are in the plural form because there are numerous areas in which we need to rule; one key (authority) for every area, but all coming from the same source! Once the decrees have been made, you 'close' the door on that issue as the work has been done.

There is one further dimension that we need to look at when functioning in the key of David and using the keys of the Kingdom of Heaven; this is the dimension of time.

Unlocking the Kairos time of God

Once again, before I continue, I would like share some definitions with you so that you may have a better understanding of the remaining part of this chapter:

Definitions according to Thayer's Greek definitions:
Kairos: a measure of time, a larger or smaller portion of time, hence: a fixed and definite time, the time when things are brought to crisis, the decisive epoch waited for; an opportue or seasonable time, the right time, a limited period of time, to what time brings, the state of the times, the things and events of time
Chronos: time either long or short. This refers to the measurement of time: seconds, minutes, hours, days, years, seasons, etc. Chronology or chronological order.

Definitions according to Webster's dictionary:
Eternal or eternity: Without beginning or end of existence.
Manifest: To show plainly, to be the evidence of, to reveal (itself) as existing. We

can also say that manifest means to make visible what always was. Something that has always been there but was not seen before is now seen. (Isa 48:1-11).

Kairos time is a spiritual time and also the 'time' that God functions with. God is beyond time, and in Him there is no beginning and no end (Rev 21:6). If we come to Him there will be eternal rest and He will give us springs of water for eternal life and sustenance (John 4:10; John 7:38). Chronos is an earthly time and the earth is governed by it. For demonstration purposes I would like to diagrammatically explain the kairos and chronos times to you:

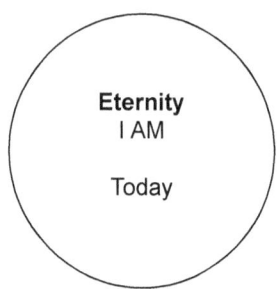

[1]Let us call the circle to the left 'eternity'. Because is without beginning or end of existence, we can also call it the vanishing point of time and it is therefore not governed by past, present and future as we know it. Therefore we can also safely say that when we speak of eternity or everlasting, we are not speaking of the future but an ageless time period, or a place not governed by chronology. When God's children pass away one day to be with Him in eternity they will move from a dimension where time (chronos) governs to a place where time vanishes. We can also call eternity 'I am', 'today' or 'spirit kairos (spirit time)', because God is the beginning and the end (Rev 21:6, Rev 22:13) and therefore beyond time; all time exists in Him.

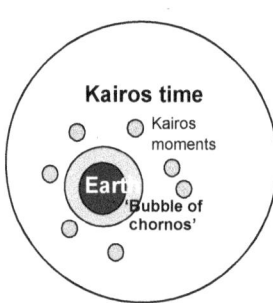

[2]When God created Adam he was placed on earth but in eternity (heavenly places or second heaven; Eph 1:3,10,20&21; Eph 2:6; Eph 6:12). This means that the first and second heavens were not separated from each other, and the earth was exposed to kairos. Adam therefore had unlimited access to the kairos moments of God for his life and destiny, which were in the spirit, even though he was living on a physical planet. God walked with Adam and Eve in the garden (Gen 3:8), into their lives.

The fall of man (Gen 3:6-11) disconnected Adam and Eve from eternity and placed them into a 'bubble', which was now governed by a 'new' time called chronos. The whole of the first heaven was from then on governed by this chronos time, which is a time that is limited because everything has a beginning and an end in chronology.

So the heavenly places were thus 'veiled' for all of mankind. Until Christ came to redeem mankind, God had to make use of specific people, the saints of the Old Testament like Moses, Samuel, Elijah, etc. to pierce this veil and draw down from the heavens the kairos moments (destiny) for the people of God; there was limited access.

---

1   Reference in these paragraphs is made to a teaching by Apostle Thamo Naidoo.

2   Reference in these paragraphs is made to a teaching by Apostle Thamo Naidoo.

We cannot determine the chronology of the time 'in the beginning', when God created heaven and earth in Genesis 1:1 because this creation was done in 'eternity' which is the vanishing point of time! Although chronos time was present from Genesis 1:4 (there was night and there was day) the earth was not governed by it until after the fall of man, because the earth was still exposed to and governed by kairos. Also keep in mind that although kairos time has a beginning and end, there is no *physical* end in God, just completion, because it is spirit time.

In our scripture of Prov 24:3&4 we have read that a house is built by wisdom, referring to the earth realm which is governed by chronos, and that it is established by understanding, which makes reference to the heavenly realm which is governed by the kairos of God, but it is by knowledge which is the ability to access the kairos moments that carry a mystery of God, that the rooms are filled with all kinds of riches.

Now, when Jesus came to earth, He not only came to restore our relationship with the Father but He also broke through the veil that was around the earth to restore our access to the kairos of God.

This happened in the following way: Jesus broke through the veil *from heaven to the earth, or from the spirit dimension to the physical dimension* at the time of His birth, when He broke through Mary's hymen, from her womb. Keep in mind that her hymen was intact until then because she was still a virgin at the time of Jesus' birth (Matt 1:22-25). Where the fall of man closed the veil to the spirit dimension from the physical dimension, Jesus now broke it from the spirit dimension into the physical dimension. There was a supernatural penetration that took place.

When Jesus was baptised the heavens were opened above Him and the Holy Spirit descended upon Him (Matt 3:16&17). From that moment on, no matter where He went, Jesus always ministered with open heavens above Him. There was no veil that limited His access to the heavens and the Father; hence the term 'open heavens'.

When Jesus yielded up His spirit and died, the temple curtain was torn from top to bottom; from the spirit dimension into the physical dimension (Matt 27:50&51). At this moment in time the veil around the earth was also torn and a way was made for the earth to be reconnected with eternity once again, making the kairos time of God accessible to mankind once more.

The scriptures say that the rocks split and the earth shook, and this happened because of the collision between the spiritual and the natural realms that took place. Every time kairos collides with chronos, there is a shaking in the physical that manifests. In Acts 4:31 the place where the disciples prayed was shaken because heaven moved toward the earth. Every time we pray God's will and Kingdom to be established on the earth, the earth will be shaken because heaven moves toward and collides with it.

After Christ's resurrection the ability to *live* in kairos was made available to all who *believed in Him*, just as Adam and Eve had lived connected to eternity. This means that just as Jesus had open heavens above Him wherever He went, so we too can have open heavens wherever we go.

The problem arises when, just as the curtain to the Holy of Holies in the temple was sewn closed after it was rent, man closes the spirit dimension again by moving in the flesh (law, tradition and sin) and not in the spirit. The religious system and religious spirit closes again that which God has opened.

Why is it so important to be able to access the kairos time of God? In every kairos moment, or epoch of time, or 'crisis' moment, there is locked up a mystery of God. This 'mystery' can be: a rhema word or revelation knowledge; a prophetic word; a Dabar word, which is the *creative life in the Word*, or *the latent power of God driving itself forward and moving toward it's fulfilment;* an aspect of God's character; blue prints of God for a nation, city, church or an individual's life; different kinds of anointing; different dimensions, and more.

At the right moment, the specific kairos needs to be manifest (to reveal itself as existing) on the earth to establish God's purpose and will for that person, church, city or nation. It is for this reason that it can also be called a crisis moment because chronos and kairos 'collide', and the Lord *manifests* what is needed on the earth from out of the spirit realm. In Rev 21:1-7 this concept is clearly explained:

> "Then I saw a new heaven and a new earth;
> for the first heaven and the first earth passed away,
> and there is no longer any sea.
>
> Rev 21:1
>
> And He who sits on the throne said,'Behold,I am making all things new.'
> And He said,'Write,for these words are faithful and true.'"
>
> Rev 21:5

1. John sees a new heaven and a new earth. In Is 65:17 the Lord says, "For behold, I create new heavens and a new earth; and the former things will not be remembered or come to mind."
    Likewise in 2 Pet 3:10-15 the Lord says that the heavens will pass away and the earth and its works will be destroyed, but He promises that we will have a new heaven and earth. So often we interpret this as a literal destruction of the heavens and the earth, but if we look at the Greek definitions we come to some very interesting insights! In both scriptures in 2 Peter and Revelation, the 'heaven' that will pass away and be new is the third heaven, as in the literal dwelling place of God. Why would God want to *destroy* His own dwelling place? This does not make sense. In 2 Pet 3:10, Peter mentions that the earth and its works will be burned up and the heavens will be destroyed. Another word that is used for destroyed is 'dissolve' which according to the Strong's concordance definition is luõ; *loo'-o*; A primary verb which means to "loosen" (literally or figuratively): -break (up), destroy, dissolve, (un-) loose, melt, put off.

In these scriptures it also speaks of heat, burning and melting. If we look in God's word we see that God is the fire (Eze 1:26-28; Mal 3:1-6; Matt 3:11&12; Acts 2:1-3; Heb 12:29; Rev 2:18). God's fire is three-fold; it is a fire of passion (priestly dimension), a fire that purifies (prophetic dimension) and it represents His glory (kingly dimension)! Therefore, when He comes He will judge all the earth and its works by fire; that which is pure will remain and the rest will be burned up (Matt 3:12).

This brings us to the next words used in these verses, being 'passed away'. The Greek word for this is 'parerchomai', pronounced *par-er'-khom-ahee*, which means to *come near or aside*, that is, to *approach* (*arrive*), *go by* (or away), (figuratively) *perish or neglect*, (causatively) *avert*: -come (forth), go, pass (away, by, over), past, transgress (Strong's concordance).

This means that there is not a literal destruction of the earth and heaven, but a passing on to something else; that 'something else' being a place where righteousness dwells (2 Pet 3:13). God is in the restoration business and He wants to restore all to its original form (Acts 3:20&21). God will 'come near' or 'aside' to execute judgement.

In Rev 21:5 the Lord says that He *is making all things new*, which is restoring them to their original created state, and NOT making all new things, which would be creating from scratch. In Rom 8:18-25 we read that all of creation is longing to be set free from the slavery and deterioration that came upon the earth at the fall of man. This is to be done through the sons of God, these being all who have received Christ as their Saviour. In 2 Cor 5:17 we see a very important link: "Therefore if anyone is in Christ, he is a new creature; the old things have passed away; behold, new things have come" (emphasis mine). The 'passed away' in 2 Cor 5:17 is the same as in Rev 21:1. When you became a child of God, He did not destroy you and make a new you. He brought you back to your original place of creation, being in His image and likeness (Gen 1:26)! You are now NEW because the OLD things have PASSED AWAY or are removed from you.

Simply said: all of creation is waiting for that which happened to you when Christ came into your life, to happen to it and you are the agent who God is using on the earth, hence the reason we need to function as kings!

Keep in mind that it is only those who are living in 'darkness' who will be taken by surprise on the day of the judgment of the Lord. The Word clearly says that we, as sons of God/light, will not be caught unawares. It will not overtake us like a thief in the night. Carefully read 1 Thessalonians 5:1-10, focusing on verses 2 to 6. We will *not know the specific hour*, only the Father knows this (Mark 13:32), but we will know that He is coming because of the intensity of stirring in our spirit man. We will sense the closeness of His presence as He 'comes near'. A bride always senses the moment when her groom approaches.

The final scripture I want to bring to your attention regarding this point is Hebrews 12:26-29. Here the Lord declares that He will once again shake not only the earth but also the heavens ('heavens' again speaking of His dwelling place). This brings us back to the question previously asked: "Why would God want to *destroy / shake* His own dwelling place?" The shaking (or burning/ destroying/passing away) is for those things that are not part of God's Kingdom and His righteousness.

"... that those things which cannot be shaken may remain." Heb 12:27b "Therefore, since we receive a kingdom which cannot be shaken ..." Heb 12:28a

We all know that the third heaven cannot be shaken or destroyed because it is part of the 'unshakable Kingdom'. Everything that is rooted in Christ and the Kingdom of God is built on a sure foundation, and when judgement comes, it will be found pure. God will 'shake' everything, including His dwelling place, to show to all, including Satan, that His Kingdom is truly unshakable and righteous. It is so awesome that we may be part of this kingdom which is unshakable and cannot be destroyed, and which is tested by God Himself who is a consuming fire (Heb 12:29)!

The reason why everything is 'new' at the end of time is simply because we have not seen what it all looked like from the beginning of creation. The 'new' heaven is because all the fullness of God will be revealed to us! When in Rev 21:4 the word says, "and He will wipe away every tear from their eyes; and there will no longer be any death; there will no longer be any mourning, or crying, or pain; the first things have passed away", it declares that there is no death (or fear of death), mourning, crying or pain, because through His life, Jesus destroyed the works of the devil; through His death He destroyed the power of the devil, and through His resurrection the fear of death was destroyed. We can now already start living in this inheritance.

The first things that have passed away makes reference to the things that we have known up to the time when Christ returns. That which was first will no longer be there, but we can have part now already of the 'new' in Christ!

> "And I saw the holy city, new Jerusalem, coming down out of heaven from God, made ready as a bride adorned for her husband."
>
> Rev 21:2

2. I would like to focus on a very important part mentioned in verse two which will give you a clear understanding of how we draw the chronos and Kairos times together, while living in the dimensions of the key of David. [3]The short phrase "Coming down out of heaven from God" makes reference to dimensions, God being the highest dimension and all comes down from Him. 'Up', 'down' or 'depth', 'in the heavens', 'on the earth' or 'under the earth' all speak of different dimensions. 'Out' always refers to origin, original or source, and therefore it also includes being revealed/manifested when 'it' comes out.

---

3 Reference in this paragraph is made to the teaching on DVD "The Key of David" by Rev. Michael Pitts

'Out of heaven' refers to the origin being the third heaven (God's presence) but also being revealed from out of the second heaven, being a spiritual dimension, into the first heaven, being the physical realm. Although the second heaven, or heavenly places, is a spiritual realm it is around us all the time, but not revealed to us. When we see angels or demons, the second heaven is being imposed onto the first heaven. Although we live in the physical realm, we have access to heavenly places because Jesus tore open the 'veil' around the first heaven. Remember that the kairos time of God is applicable in the second and third heavens.

So, in this scripture, the new Jerusalem is coming down from the Lord in the third heaven, being a dimension, and it is also coming 'out of heaven' (heavenly places), meaning that it is revealed to us in the physical. (Also see Rev 3:12&13. Refer to Chapter number two also, page twenty nine, concerning Jerusalem.) We see that here in Revelation, the new Jerusalem is now not only in us, but brought out to us as a totally new dimension and also a literal dwelling place for the end of the ages (Heb 11:13-16).

In the same way, Jesus came down out of heaven from God. Jesus was sent by the Father (origin) and He was revealed (out) to us in the physical. We can say that He is the Father or 'I AM', revealed. Jesus allowed us to see different characteristics of God the Father:
- I AM the bread of life – John 6:35,48,51
- I AM the light of the world – John 8:12
- I AM the gate – John 10:7-9
- I AM the good shepherd – John 10:11&14
- I AM the resurrection and the life – John 11:25
- I AM the way and the truth and the life – John 14:6
- I AM the true vine – John 15:1&5.

In the same way we can consider the kairos moments: A kairos (crisis) moment comes *down from God (containing a mystery of God)* and out of heaven (*manifests on earth*). We, as sons of God, are to take hold of the kairos moments and draw them onto the earth so that they will manifest in the chronos time! Remember that God has called us to be sons and not servants, and because we are sons we have an inheritance; we are co-heirs with Christ (Rom 8:17; Rev 21:7). When a kairos moment manifests, God's will penetrates into the earth and manifests in the physical. When Eph 2:6 says that we are seated with Christ in heavenly places it makes reference to this very principle too. Heb 11:13 says that we are strangers on this earth, the reason being that we are called to be seated with Christ in heavenly places, as we are primarily spirit beings.

As Jesus has already rent the veil around the earth, we no longer have to pierce the veil and pull down the kairos moments from the heavens onto the earth, like the saints of the Old Testament did, but we, being seated in heavenly places with Christ, push down from the spirit dimension onto the earth, because of our heavenly position which we obtain as we function as priests! It is much easier to push something down than to pull it down to establish it. A builder always builds from the top, never from the bottom.

We have been so used to calling on God and pulling things down from heaven and we have exhausted ourselves in doing so. Most of our time and energy is spent in doing this, and yet we do not see full results. However, the Lord is calling us to be with Him, spending most of our time and energy with Him in the heavenly places in His presence, where He will give us the tools and reveal 'crisis moments' to us, so that we may establish them on the earth.

In order for us to receive the full kairos moments, being for our own lives or that of the Kingdom of Heaven on earth, we need to be positioned in the second heaven, as we can only break through the second veil to the third heavens (where the decrees are spoken and released) from this position. This is achieved through functioning in the dimensions of the priest and prophet. When you function in your kingly dimension on earth, you move in 'open heavens' and the work you do is almost effortless. You are therefore 'coming down from God', taking the kairos mystery with you, and 'out of heaven', manifesting on the earth in chronos that kairos of God.

Also keep in mind that when we are positioned in heavenly places, not only can we hear the decrees that are spoken in the third heaven, but we can clearly see where we need to function as kings on the earth because we see God moving in that area.

It is when we come to this point that the supernatural breaks out in our lives, and we can see into the third heaven like Isaiah and Ezekiel (Isa 6:1-7; Eze 1:1-28), or we are taken up into the heavenly realm like Paul (2 Cor 12:2-4) and John (Rev 4:1&2). We will be enabled by the Lord to move in the spirit like Elisha (2 Kings 5:25), Philip (Acts 8:38-40) and Paul (Col 2:5). Remember that all these people moved in the supernatural because there was a specific purpose to be effected for the Kingdom of God. Everything that God allows us to do in the supernatural, being healing, casting out of demons, prayer, sharing the word, etc is always for the **purpose** of the **expansion of His Kingdom** and **never** to show how 'great' we are or just for the sake of 'moving in the supernatural'!

> "... 'Behold, the tabernacle of God is among men, and He will dwell among them, and they shall be His people, and God Himself will be among them."
>
> Rev 21:3

3. Jesus is the tabernacle of God and He firstly seeks to dwell in the tabernacle of your heart. God wants to dwell, not visit, with His people. This has been His desire from the beginning (Gen 3:8) and one day He will dwell with us again in His fullness as He did then.

Teach me to number my days

> "So teach us to number our days,
> That we may present to You a heart of wisdom.
>
> Ps 90:12

Also read Ps 39:4. When Moses said "teach us to number our days" he was asking God to teach/give him the ability to access the kairos moments for each day of his life. Remember that your destiny is locked up in kairos (Acts 17:26) and therefore this should be your prayer too! The second part of this verse (Ps 90:12) is just as awesome: That we may present to God a heart of wisdom once again speaks about the ability to function on the earth in the kingly dimension, for which we need wisdom to establish what we have received, once we have tapped into the kairos of God.

At this point I would like to make one clear differentiation. The ability to tap into and interpret the full, deeper mysteries of God for the church is an apostolic grace. These deeper mysteries will be released and opened up to the body by an apostolic (five-fold) minister at the correct time. This is why the apostolic ministry is of utmost importance in the body of Christ so that the revelations of Christ can be released and established in the body to mature it. Now, there is within that new dimension that has been released, all the kairos moments that the church needs to access for kingdom life! So we can say that an apostle breaks open and the people live in that dimension but you are responsible to access your destiny!

Let us look at Ex 23:20-33 to see how this works:

- "Behold, I am going to send an angel before you to guard you along the way and to bring you into the place which I have prepared. Be on your guard before him and obey his voice; do not be rebellious toward him, for he will not pardon your transgression since My name is in him. But if you truly obey his voice and do all that I say, then I will be an enemy to your enemies and an adversary to your adversaries." Ex 23:20-22

When God says that He will 'bring you into the *place* [that He has] prepared' He is speaking of bringing you into your destiny! God will guide you to reach your destiny, but you need to realise that you need to become active to attain it. Your priestly function is to hear God's voice and draw near to Him so that He may reveal this 'place' or destiny to you. God will also 'not pardon transgression' and we need to know that even though God's grace is abundant for us there will always be a consequence for disobedience. The maximum length of the 'season' you are in is always linked to your obedience to the Lord; the minimum length is determined by God. You will find that your obedience will release the breakthrough in certain situations you find yourself in. Do not always blame the enemy if things go wrong in your life; it may just simply be your disobedience causing the circumstance, or God may be teaching you something (My name is in Him).

- "For my angel will go before you and bring you to the land of the Amorites …; and I will completely destroy them. You shall not worship their gods, nor serve them, nor do according to their deeds; but you shall utterly overthrow them and break their sacred pillars in pieces." Ex 23:23&24

    You are called to take in territories, which are those things that the Lord has promised you. All the 'ites' that you come across are those things that are hindrances to you, and you need to overcome them in order to take full possession of your land. Tear down all strongholds that are elevated above God in your life, so that you may have complete reign in that which God has destined you for.

- "But you shall serve the Lord your God, and He will bless your bread and your water; and I will remove sickness from your midst. There shall be no one miscarrying or barren in your land; I will fulfil the number of your days." Ex 23:25&26

    As you serve God alone and no other idols (compromise) He will bless you in the following areas: Your bread will be blessed which speaks of the revelation of the Word you will receive; your water will be blessed meaning that you will always have connection and flow of life to the Holy Spirit; all form of sickness will be removed from your body, soul or spirit! You will be fruitful in every area of your life (no barrenness) and there will always be a full term served (no miscarrying) in that what you do and the work (or seed) of each area will be manifested. All you do will prosper and bear fruit.

    o   Expanding upon the phrase 'I will fulfil the number of your days' we take a look at Eph 1:7-12. God will fulfil your days as He intended but you first need to come to Christ for redemption and forgiveness, then you will see the riches of His grace for your life (verses 7&8).

    o   There are certain mysteries (kairos moments) pertaining to your life that the Lord wants you to tap into so that you can come into the fullness of your purpose in Him; the purpose that He has planned and that He desires for you. You can, through Christ, tap into the kairos of God and establish on the earth the dimensions made available to you (verses 8&9).

    o   The word 'administration' in verse ten, according to Webster's dictionary, means to manage as a steward or executor. You have to administrate or steward the kairos that God makes available and releases to you. If you do not administrate the 'crisis moments' accurately in your life, you will not be allowed to access more in the heavens. It is important that you know the 'fullness of the times' or what dimension of time God is releasing. This means that with each kairos or crisis moment, there is not just a mystery of God concealed in it, but also a specific dimension of time or season for that kairos which is released or accessed to be made manifest on the earth (verse 10). See 'Discerning the times of God and what to do in them' following this section.

    o   You have been predestined (destiny) to work according to His dream for you! Through all the revelation and abundance that God brings to you, you must realise that you are part of a bigger picture that God sees. He will therefore bring you into connection with the bigger picture so that His Kingdom can be made manifest and established (verses 11&12).

- "I will send My terror ahead of you, and throw into confusion all the people among whom you come, and I will make all your enemies turn their backs to you. I will send hornets ahead of you …
  I will not drive them out before you in a single year, that the land may not become desolate and the beasts of the field become too numerous for you. I will drive them out before you little by little, until you become fruitful and take possession of the land." Ex 23:27-30
  God will drive out the enemy before you but you need to identify what God is doing and follow His leading. There may be many areas in which God is working in your life, but you cannot run ahead of Him. He will not deal with everything all at once, because if He does and you receive your 'land' all at once, your capacity may be too small for the responsibility that God gives you, and you will not be able to administrate it correctly. God needs to enlarge your spirit capacity so that you can receive the fullness of the measure that He has for you (Eph 3:19). This He will do little by little to give you room to grow so that you are not overwhelmed. The Lord wants you to be fruitful, which is the ability to multiply / increase your capacity, and then tend to what He has given to you.
  - You need to remember the order of things: New work cannot be built on religious systems but only on Godly revelation (Matt 9:16&17).

- "I will fix your boundary … for I will deliver the inhabitants of the land into your hand, and you will drive them out before you. You shall make no covenant with them or with their gods.
  They shall not live in your land, because they will make you sin against Me; for if you serve their gods, it will surely be a snare to you." Ex 23:31-33
  God has fixed the dimensions we are to walk in, but it is our responsibility to walk in them. Too often we want God to do everything for us, but we need to realise that if we do not do our part nothing will happen. The Lord closes off this passage by again stressing the importance that we should not worship idols because it will cause us to fall. If we function within the boundaries the Lord has set for us, we will have success and favour!

Discerning the times of God and what to do in them

It is vital that we discern the kairos times of God for the specific chronos that we are facing! Then, once we know the time or 'season', we will know what to do in that time. The word says, "Of the sons of Issachar, men who understood the times, with knowledge of what Israel should do …" I Chron 12:32. If we do not know the times we do not know what to do with what we have available! Together with the mystery of God and the dimension of time, authority (keys) to move and do according to what is given in that dimension is also released. Notice how the men understood the times (priestly dimension) and had knowledge (prophetic dimension) of what should be done (kingly dimension)!

Ecc 3:1-8 is a scripture that is often quoted to denounce chronos time, especially at funerals. If we take a closer look at these verses we see that there is, however, a totally different meaning that comes to light. There is an appointed time or season (an *appointed* occasion) in the spirit (kairos) and in the physical (chronos), and these times need to be brought together to establish God's Kingdom on earth. There is also a purpose for every activity that is done. The 'negative' and 'positive' in verses 2 to 8 always relate to one another, and are used in conjunction with one another. Let us take a closer look at this.

Verse two deals with **identity**, being identity both of oneself and the identity of the body of Christ.

To be born:
- One is not just born physically but there is a spiritual birth that needs to take place (1 Pet 1:23). Together with this, there is a raising or bringing of sons into the Kingdom of Heaven.
- There is also a birthing that takes place in the spirit realm where things are brought forth or manifested.
- Finally there is a start of something new, being physically in your life, for example a new occupation, or a new season that you enter in spiritually.

To die:
- Besides the obvious physical death there is also the spiritual death, which does not just apply here on earth but also in eternity for those who choose to deny Christ.
- By our words and attitudes or lack of faith we can cause 'abortions' to take place in the spirit realm. Spiritual abortions are basically preventing something to break through in the spirit and therefore it will also not manifest on the earth.
- Finally there is an ending, completion of something or a full cycle that something has run.

To plant:
- There needs to be a planting into your heart, which is placing the foundations of Christ in your spirit. Your identity is directly related to the revelation you have of Christ (Who is Christ – Who am I).
- Renew your mind through the seed of God's word that is planted in your mind (Rom 12:2). The more God's word is planted in you, the stronger your mind becomes, and the easier it is to resist the enemy!
- As you have the seed of God's word planted in your life, and it grows through revelation of that seed, so you will find that you are able to establish patterns that will move you to victory!

To uproot:
- The moment you are reborn, the sinful nature that is in you is taken out! This leaves you with sinful habits that you can easily deal with as the Lord brings them to your attention.
- You further need to eradicate all incorrect thought patterns, paradigms, false beliefs and cycles of defeat (Rom 12:2). These things need to be ruthlessly uprooted so that the seed of God's word can be planted in you and take root!

- You also need to uproot all incorrect attitudes that have established themselves in your heart.

Verse three deals with the aspect of **establishing the Kingdom of God**. Keep in mind that the Kingdom firstly needs to be established in our lives before we can establish it around us.

To kill:
- We need to 'kill' everything that feeds the enemy in our lives. All dealings of the flesh like selfishness, pride, jealousy, hypocrisy, immorality and discord need to be eliminated from our lives, because it is through these things that the enemy can establish his kingdom, not just in our lives, but in society too.
- We also need to address the area of wrong motivations: Everything that is not motivated by the Holy Spirit will result in dead works and will bear no fruit in God's Kingdom.

To heal:
- Part of establishing God's Kingdom is to bring restoration to the lives of people. God's desire is to bring back people from brokenness and loss of purpose to the original design, and set them on course for destiny. We are His instruments in this restoration process.
- The second part of healing is bringing the body of Christ to a place of wholeness in Him. The bride's identity is being restored, and the Lord is moving us from imperfection to perfection, as He will come for a pure and spotless bride (Eph 5:27).

To tear (Break) down:
- Any reasoning, imagination, thought, attitude or barrier that has set itself up against the knowledge of Christ must be torn down (2 Cor 10:5). We cannot tolerate negative thought patterns and doctrines that cause God's people to go astray.
- We remove all demonic entities that occupy the atmosphere that have taken root in our lives, as we have allowed them to do so because of the thoughts and sins we are guilty of. In the same way in which you allow weeds to grow, so the demonic forces will also grow if they are not addressed.
- We also tear down every work of the enemy and his plans.
  - Please note: it is important that you function in the area of authority that the Lord has given you. Not every person is called to address Principalities and Powers in the atmosphere directly. You can pray for situations, but don't just go around binding demonic entities in areas over which you have no authority!

To build (up):
- We continue to build on what has been planted into our lives. This is a progressive building upon the revelation of Christ and a maturing of our inner man. As we mature, we grow in our sonship.
- We need to build into the spirit atmosphere to establish God's kingdom before it manifests on the earth. This building consists of declarations of God's

word and prophetic word that the Lord has released, until the atmosphere is saturated. In Matt 11:12 it says that the violent take the Kingdom by force.
- We cannot passively wait for something to happen. God wants us to be active.
  o Please note: very often we first need to build the decrees of the Lord into the spirit atmosphere before we tear down demonic entities, so that once the demonic is gone, there is something to fill the 'gap', or else the situation will worsen (Matt 12:43-45).

In verse four we gain more understanding about the times of **intercession**.
Weep:
- There is a time in which we weep before the Lord, in order to make known to God the burdens of our heart. These are burdens of the spirit man and speak of heaviness of load that we carry because of circumstances in our lives (Ps 55:22; Matt 11:30). One can almost say that we are laying our complaint about a specific thing before the Lord.
- Further we call to God and weep on behalf of others in prayer and intercession, for the circumstances in their lives.

Laugh:
- We laugh at the enemy and bring him to a place of disgrace and defeat. This laughing is born out of a knowledge of who we are in Christ, and that through Him we are victorious. Once we have the revelation of victory, we laugh at the plans of the enemy.
- It literally means to tease the enemy, however not in disrespect, but in a manner of showing his loss as we gain the victory in Christ. This is the Lord laughing through us at the enemy!

Mourn:
- To mourn is a deeper level of intercession than to weep (See the definitions at the end of this chapter). It is being burdened for someone or for a situation that people are in. You are so burdened that you 'feel' the weight of the situation. You travail before the Lord continuously until the breakthrough comes, no matter how long it takes!
- To mourn also means to be burdened with the Lord's heart, or to be heavy with His heart. God's heart is imposed upon ours and we experience a tiny part of what He experiences. This then moves us to intercede until this burden lifts from us.

Dance:
- Once the breakthrough has come, we come to a state of celebration because of victory in the situation / over the enemy. There is an exuberant rejoicing in God and what He has done. When this level of celebration breaks out, it is often expressed through the body by jumping or leaping and shouting.
- To dance also means that we are living in a place of victory. Victory is not just celebrated when it happens; we need to live in a state of victory. Too often we do not do this, and the enemy comes to steal again.

Verse five speaks of *taking up* and *laying down* of **authority and responsibility**. Stones speak of weight, symbolising responsibility. Stones are used to build with but they can also be instruments of destruction.

Scatter (cast away):
- This speaks of refusing responsibility in that which you are not called to do, because you can easily bring destruction if you are not called to do what you are doing. Remember that you are not responsible for everything that comes your way. As children of God we need to make mature decisions and need to learn how to say 'no' if what we are asked to do is not our area of functioning, or God is not leading us into that specific thing. Gather together:
- You must take up responsibility in the area in which you are called. Taking up responsibility comes along with accepting responsibility when things go wrong too, and dealing with that issue. People will respect you for that. Remember that with rank or position comes responsibility. Too often people want the title but not the responsibility that goes with it; you can never separate the two.
- As you take up your responsibility in an area, you will start functioning in the authority that God has given you in that area. Responsibility and authority go hand in hand.

Embrace:
- Embracing refers to accepting a certain situation and then dealing with it in a godly way. There are times that we just need to accept what is happening, and as we start dealing with the situations, God will teach us valuable lessons and guide us through them. Jesus went through the storm with His disciples, not around it (Mark 4:35-41).
- Lastly there is a 'binding to' or commitment that is made to people or a certain activity. This binding does not merely refer to a normal commitment, but speaks of covenant, which leads to destiny. God made a covenant with Abraham, Isaac and Jacob (Ex 2:24) and numerous other people, including the church (Heb 12:24), and in all this there was a destiny involved. A covenant is not something to be taken lightly.

Refrain from:
- You need to refrain from getting involved in certain situations or activities that will influence you negatively. You need to discern those things that will draw you down and then refrain from that activity or situation.
- To refrain from also means to disconnect yourself from something. Don't be committed to something that is not of God or that He has no part of. If you are going to represent the Kingdom, there are certain things you cannot be part of or associated with. It is then not a matter of people accepting you or not but a matter of Kingdom representation or miss-representation.

The aspect of **relationship** is revealed in verse six.
Search (gain/get):
- Primarily you are to search out or come into relationship with the Lord. You need to seek Him (Jer 29:13; Ps 145:19) and desire Him only, like a wife desires

her husband (Matt 6:33). If you do not have the 'vertical' relationship intact, you will never be able to have a 'horizontal' relationship with your fellow man. Relationship with the Lord is the foundation on which your whole life rests!
- At times you need to seek counsel or advice (Jer 33:3) being either primarily from the Lord, or from people who have the necessary training in a certain area. It does not help to seek advice from someone who does not know what he/she is doing, as this would constitute foolishness.

Loose (Give up):
- You are to loose yourself and be of no reputation in the eyes of the Lord. Being of no reputation does not speak of denying who God created you to be but rather speaks of humility before the Lord. It is our responsibility to remain humble; Jam 4:10 says, "Humble yourselves in the presence of the Lord and He will exalt you."
- You must also give up unrighteous relationships that hinder you in your relationship with God. Too often we allow ourselves to be connected with people whose only interest is to bring a wedge between the Lord and us, drawing us further and further away from Him. These are the relationships that we either need to break with completely, or distance ourselves from, depending on the situation.

Keep:
- You are to primarily keep the 'flame' of passion alive that God has set in your heart. Hold on to what God has given you from His word, and keep and walk the destiny He has given you.
- As sons of God we are called to be keepers of the flame. This is a flame of passion, purity and promise that is to burn brightly in our lives so that all can see we know the Lord. Being flame keepers also means that we must distribute the flame and allow it to spread where we go. Many times we 'keep' the flame so within us, that the people do not even know that we have a flame! To keep does not just mean to retain but to 'tend to' or 'attend to'.
- To keep also means to watch for or to be a watchman for God concerning His people. Although this refers to intercession, this aspect of 'keeping' involves protecting and 'hedging in' the people of the Lord. In order to do this you need to be in relationship with the people you are 'hedging in'! This protection includes warning, and giving wisdom and guidance (Isa 62:6&7).

Cast (throw) away:
- It is necessary to cast out every idol of the heart and remove it from your temple. Idols will hinder your relationship with God. No one can serve two masters, as one will always be favoured (Matt 6:24). You must cast out every enemy of God in your life.
- There needs to be a casting away of every offence and reproach in your life because this will bring division and strife if you allow it to remain. Offence does not belong in the body of Christ, and it is one of the enemy's greatest weapons that brings division. Many times offence comes into your heart because you have the issue that needs to be dealt with!

In verse seven the **authority of the Word** is explained.

Tear (rend):
- The sword of the word brings division according to Heb 4:12. This means that as the word of God comes into your heart it will bring separation between your thoughts and the thoughts of God. There is a removing of your own thoughts and they are replaced by God's word. Separation in general can be positive and negative but when the word comes it brings alignment.
- In Is 61:1 it says that we will bring good news to the afflicted. This is done through the word of God. He will give us words that will take people out of their current afflictions and bring them into the new of God's word. We underestimate the power of God's word, and we need to start using His word to tear people from the situations that they are in so that they can move in freedom. The judgment of God comes upon their circumstances as we speak His word.
- Even as we speak against spirits of deception that hold people captive, these people will receive freedom as the deceptions are torn from them by God's word of truth.

Mend (sew):
- The word of God will mend or sew your heart together with His heart and destiny for your life. When His word flows it reveals His desires and promises for His children and draws them closer to Him.
- The word will cause mending of broken relationships and the repairing of what has been torn through strife and discord between people and churches; there is a coming back to, or a place of joining or being part of the body. God's word brings unity, for everything is built on the foundation of Christ who is the word (Ps 133:1&2; John 1:1).
- Isaiah 61 declares that there will be a mending of those with broken hearts as the word of the Lord brings healing to their hearts. The word has the power to mend or remake people's spirits.

Silent:
- Psalm 46:10 declares that we are to 'be still and know that [He is] God'. This means that you need to be at rest in your spirit, being content that after He has spoken His word and you have done what it requires, you know that it will go forth and establish what God has said (Is 55:11).
- There are times and situations when we are not to speak, but to remain silent before people and even the enemy. Too often we want to defend others or ourselves, and we end up bringing more confusion and hurt. Know when to keep silent and allow God to vindicate you (Is 54:17).

Speak:
- We are to speak on God's behalf and declare His word to the nations, tribes and tongues. We need not fear, because He is with us, and we must move in boldness, proclaiming His word. We must use wisdom when speaking to people and into situations.
- The church is to build into the spirit atmosphere by proclaiming the word that God has spoken in a specific situation. You are to create by speaking the

Word because there is creative life in the Word of God, which has the power to bring forth. As you speak, God's power is released and it drives itself forward coming to its fulfilment and establishing what it has been sent to do.
- There are times when you need to speak out to subdue your circumstances, the enemy, demonic spirits, etc. When the time comes to speak, do not keep silent but speak in boldness and authority and you will see the enemy defeated.

Finally, verse eight speaks of **exercising your dominion** on the earth.

Love:
- Firstly you need to love the people of the earth, accepting who they are and who God has created them to be (John 13:34&35). No matter from what tribe, tongue or nation; all people are created in God's image and likeness and carry His seal of approval upon them.
- You must learn to extend your hand in friendship to God's creation (people). Only when you truly love people, you can reach their hearts with God's love, and barriers between man and God can fall. Never judge the person!
- There will be some people with whom you will enter into covenant because these are the people who are connected with you in destiny, and you have a vital role to play in each others' lives. Extend friendship to all people but be covenanted to only those who God shows you!

Hate:
- We are to hate the enemy and what He does (1 Peter 5:8&9; 1 Thess 5:22; 3 John 1:11) without exception.
- Hate the wrong deeds of people and their sin (1 Thess 5:15). It is important that you separate the person from the sin; this is what God does. God hates sin but He still loves the people who commit the sin. If this were not so we would be in a serious predicament!

War:
- There is a time where we are to make war with the enemy and to overcome and prevail against him. Ignoring him will not win the battles! This includes engaging in battle and being victorious over circumstances, demonic harassment, illness and any situation that the enemy brings against us. It is God who protects us (Ps 32:7), but we are to fight (2 Cor 10:4&5; Eph 6:10-12). Passivity toward the enemy is one of the biggest dangers.

Peace:
- Peace is not just being at rest in your spirit, but also being at peace with all who are around you. If you don't war you cannot come into rest (Rom 16:19&20).
- Peace or shalom, does not just mean rest but encompasses completeness, favour, good health, peace, prosperity, rest and welfare in your entire life. The completeness of every facet of the life of abundance that Christ came to give you (John 10:10) is available to you. You do not spend your entire life in the war zone; even a soldier will go home to rest!

Now looking at the times, as explained above, you need to identify what dimension of time is released within your position of relationship, revelation and rulership. One very important aspect that needs to be highlighted here is that God's time (kairos) may not necessarily make rational sense when you are to impose it into the chronos. For example: you may find yourself in a situation where you need to defend yourself but the Lord clearly denies you to speak. Know that God knows what kairos is needed to penetrate into your situation to bring victory.

There are so many stories related in the Bible where God seemed to give instructions that did not make sense but in the end brought the breakthrough! To mention but a few: Joshua and Jericho (Josh 6); Gideon overcoming Midian with 300 men (Judg 7); David and Goliath (1 Sam 17:31-52).

I believe that at this point you are able to see how the key of David and the keys of the Kingdom of Heaven function and how, by adding this dimension of time, you can not only function in what God has given you to do, but you can also function accurately.

DEFINITIONS USED IN CHAPTER SEVEN

These definitions are taken from Strong's concordance.

Verse two:
Born: ya^lad; *yaw-lad'*. To bear young; to beget; medically to act as midwife; specifically to *show lineage*: -bear, beget, birth ([-day]), (make to) bring forth (children, young), bring up, calve, child, come, be delivered (of a child), time of delivery, gender, hatch, labour, (do the office of a) midwife, declare pedigrees, be the son of, (woman in, woman that) travail (-eth, -ing woman).
Die: mu^th; *mooth*. To *die* (literally or figuratively); to *kill*: (be) dead (body, man, one), (put to, worthy of) death, destroy (-er), (cause to, be like to, must) die, kill, slay, very suddenly.
Plant: na^ta; *naw-tah'* . Properly to *strike* in, that is, *fix*; specifically to *plant* (literally or figuratively): - fastened, plant (-er).
Uproot: a^qar; *aw-kar'*. To *pluck* up (especially by the roots); specifically to hamstring; figuratively to exterminate: - dig down, hough, pluck up, root up.

Verse three:
Kill: ha^rag; *haw-rag'*. To smite with deadly intent: -destroy, out of hand, kill, murder (-er), put to [death], make [slaughter], slay (-er).
Heal: ra^pha^'; *raw-faw'*. Properly to *mend* (by stitching), that is, (figuratively) to cure: - cure, (cause to) heal, physician, repair, thoroughly, make whole.
Tear (Break) down: pa^rats; *paw-rats'*. To *break* out (in many applications, direct and indirect, literally and figuratively): -X abroad, (make a) breach, break (away, down, -er, forth, in, up), burst out, come (spread) abroad, compel, disperse, grow, increase, open, press, scatter, urge.
Build (up): ba^na^h; *baw-naw'*. To *build* (literally and figuratively): -(begin to) build (-er), obtain children, make, repair, set (up), X surely.

Verse four:
Weep: ba^ka^h; *baw-kaw'*. To *weep*; generally to bemoan: -X at all, bewail, complain, make lamentation (contention, X more, mourn, X sore, X with tears, weep.
Laugh: s´a^chaq; *saw-khak'*. To *laugh* (in pleasure or detraction); by implication to play: -deride, have in derision, laugh, make merry, mock (-er), play, rejoice, (laugh to) scorn, be in (make) sport.
Mourn: sa^phad; *saw-fad'*. Properly to *tear* the hair and *beat* the breasts (as Orientals do in grief); generally to *lament*; by implication to *wail*: -lament, mourn (-er), wail.
Dance: ra^qad; *raw-kad'*. Properly to *stamp*, that is, to *spring* about (wildly or for joy): - dance, jump, leap, skip.

Verse five:
Stones: 'eben; *eh'-ben*. From the root of H1129 through the meaning, to *build*; a *stone*: -+ carbuncle, + mason, + plummet, [chalk-, hail-, bead-, sling-] stone (ny),

(divers) weight (-s).
Scatter (cast away): sha^lak; *shaw-lak'*. To *throw* out, down or away (literally or figuratively): - adventure, cast (away, down, forth, off, out), hurl, pluck, throw.
Gather together: ka^nas; *kaw-nas'*. To *collect*; hence, to *enfold*: -gather (together), heap up, wrap self.
Embrace: cha^baq; *khaw-bak'*. To clasp (the hands or in embrace): -embrace, fold.
Refrain from: ra^chaq; *raw-khak'*. To *widen* (in any direction), that is, (intransitively) *recede* or (transitively) *remove* (literally or figuratively, of place or relation): -(a, be, cast, drive, get, go, keep [self], put, remove, be too, [wander], withdraw) far (away, off), loose, X refrain, very, (be) a good way (off).

Verse six:
Search (gain/get): ba^qash; *baw-kash'*. To *search* out (by any method; specifically in worship or prayer); by implication to *strive* after: -ask, beg, beseech, desire, enquire, get, make inquisition, procure, (make) request, require, seek (for).
Loose (Give up): 'a^bad; *aw-bad'*. Properly to *wander* away, that is *lose* oneself; by implication to *perish* (causatively, destroy): -break, destroy (-uction), + not escape, fail, lose, (cause to, make) perish, spend, X and surely, take, be undone, X utterly, be void of, have no way to flee.
Keep: sha^mar; *shaw-mar'*. Properly to *hedge* about (as with thorns), that is, *guard*; generally to *protect*, *attend* to, etc.: -beware, be circumspect, take heed (to self), keep (-er, self), mark, look narrowly, observe, preserve, regard, reserve, save (self), sure, (that lay) wait (for), watch (-man).
Cast (throw) away: sha^lak; *shaw-lak'*. To *throw* out, down or away (literally or figuratively): - adventure, cast (away, down, forth, off, out), hurl, pluck, throw.

Verse seven:
Tear (rend): qa^ra; *kaw-rah'*. To *rend*, literally or figuratively (revile, paint the eyes, as if enlarging them): - cut out, rend, X surely, tear.
Mend (sew): ta^phar; *taw-far'*. To sew: - (women that) sew (together).
Silent: cha^sha^h; *khaw-shaw'*. To *hush* or keep quiet: -hold peace, keep silence, be silent, (be) still.
Still: ra^pha^h; *raw-faw'*. To *slacken* (in many applications, literally or figuratively): -abate, cease, consume, draw [toward evening], fail, (be) faint, be (wax) feeble, forsake, idle, leave, let alone (go, down), (be) slack, stay, be still, be slothful, (be) weak (-en).
Speak: da^bar; *daw-bar'*. Perhaps properly to *arrange*; but used figuratively (of words) to *speak*; rarely (in a destructive sense) to *subdue*: -answer, appoint, bid, command, commune, declare, destroy, give, name, promise, pronounce, rehearse, say, speak, be spokesman, subdue, talk, teach, tell, think, use [entreaties], utter, X well, X work.

Verse eight:
Love: 'a^hab 'a^he^b; *aw-hab'*, *aw-habe'*. To have *affection* for (sexually or otherwise): - (be-) love (-d, -ly, -r), like, friend.

Hate: s´a^ne^'; *saw-nay'*. To *hate* (personally): -enemy, foe, (be) hate (-ful, -r), odious, X utterly.

War: milcha^ma^h; *mil-khaw-maw'*. From H3898 (in the sense of *fighting*); a *battle* (that is, the *engagement*); generally *war* (that is, *warfare*): -battle, fight, (ing), war ([-rior]). la^cham; *law-kham'*. To feed on; figuratively to consume; by implication to battle (*as destruction*): -devour, eat, X ever, fight (-ing), overcome, prevail, (make) war (-ring).

Peace: sha^lo^m; *shaw-lome'*. From H7999; *safe*, that is, (figuratively) *well, happy, friendly*; also (abstractly) *welfare*, that is, health, prosperity, peace: -X do, familiar, X fare, favour, + friend, X greet, (good) health, (X perfect, such as be at) peace (-able, -ably), prosper (-ity, -ous), rest, safe (-ly), salute, welfare, (X all is, be) well, X wholly.

sha^lam; *shaw-lam'*. To *be safe* (in mind, body or estate); figuratively to be (causatively *make*) *completed*; by implication to *be friendly*; by extension to reciprocate (in various applications): -make amends, (make an) end, finish, full, give again, make good, (re-) pay (again), (make) (to) (be at) peace (-able), that is perfect, perform, (make) prosper (-ous), recompense, render, requite, make restitution, restore, reward, X surely.

APPLICATION STUDY GUIDE FOR CHAPTER SEVEN

1. Do you fully understand the dimension of functioning in the times of God? Take time to allow the Holy Spirit to solidify these principles in your mind and spirit by:
   a. Reading the chapter or parts of the chapter that you are uncertain about again.
   b. Studying the following scriptures:
      - Josh 5:2&9
      - Ps 69:13
      - Ps 102:13
      - John 13:1-3
      - Matt 26:45, Mark 14:41
      - 1 Cor 4:5

2. Eph 2:6 says that we 'are seated with Christ in heavenly places'. Are you positioned correctly in the spirit with Christ? If yes, what is the evidence that can be seen in your life? What shifts do you need to make to come into the correct position?
3. How is your life affected by the kairos of God and how do you react to this kairos?
4. Are you positioned correctly, not just in your relationship with God, but in the destiny He has set for you? Can you access the kairos for your life, and if not, what does the Lord want you to do to correct this?
5. Are you able to accurately discern the times of God and what to do in them? If not, what does the Lord want you to do to become more accurate in your discernment?

Pray with me:

"Lord help me to discern the times like the sons of Issachar could, who had understanding of these times with knowledge of what to do. Lord teach me to number my days so that I will live in the fullness that You have ordained for my life, and that I may reach the winning line without being disqualified.

I declare that I will be able to move in the times that You show me, and that I will be accurate in all I do in Your Kingdom.

Jesus I ask for Your 'shalom' to manifest in my life. Amen."

CHAPTER EIGHT

MOVING INTO THE ORDER OF MELCHIZEDEK

God has intended for us to function in the priestly, prophetic (perceiving) and kingly role from the beginning of time, not just in our 'Christian walk' at church, but also in our daily 'living'. We cannot separate Christ from His body and we are part of that body! No matter where you go or where you are, He is right there with you. When you go to eat, your leg cannot say, "I am not hungry therefore I will stay here". In much the same way, we cannot say to the Lord: "I am going to work, so please stay at home Jesus until it is time for church".

We have separated Jesus from our family lives, our work, our social lives and sometimes even from our 'church'. It is time that we step into the fullness that God has for us and this will mean that we include Him in everything we do!

Melchizedek, king of Salem, was a prophetic preview not just of Christ (Heb 6:19&20) but of the way we are to live. Directly after Melchizedek was revealed as a priest in Gen 14, the Lord referred to Abraham as a prophet when He spoke to Abimelech, king of Gerar in Gen 20. In Ex 25 God established the Aaronnic priesthood, the Levitical order and revealed, in part, what the heavens contain through the Tabernacle of Moses.

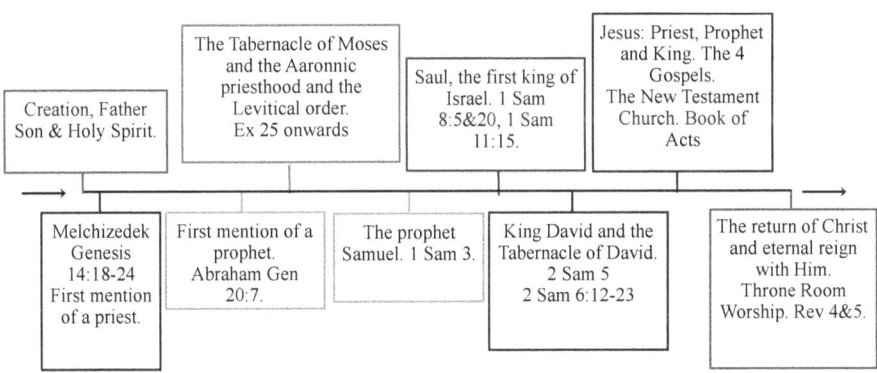

It is interesting to see how the priestly and prophetic dimensions are revealed just about simultaneously but it is only in 1 Sam 11 that the first king of Israel is crowned, revealing the kingly dimension. In 2 Sam David is crowned king of Israel but he reveals all three dimensions, previously only revealed by Melchizedek and the prophet Samuel. David returns the Ark of the Lord to Jerusalem and his tabernacle becomes a prophetic preview of Throne Room Worship that is expressed in Rev 4&5; a further revelation for Israel from God's heart.

After 400 years of silence Jesus the great priest, prophet and king is revealed to the world and creation. We see how God taught His people step by step how to live, firstly as priests and prophets, and then, once they functioned in these dimensions, He revealed the kingly dimension to them. In Jesus all these are drawn together again to bring a full circle.

The church today is still 'stuck' in functioning in the Aaronnic priesthood, something that is no longer applicable because Christ has risen from the dead and paid the price for our sins. This sacrifice is paid once and for all and will never have to be repeated. It is for this reason that Heb 7:11-17 mentions that, if another priesthood arises, then the law needs to change. Jesus came to fulfil the law and therefore met all its requirements. There is now a change in the way things operate: we are governed by grace! Heb 7:28 says that the law appoints men as high priests but the word of the oath, in this case God's word and promise to reconcile man to God, appointed the Son to do this work.

> "For it is attested of Him, 'You are a priest forever according to the order of Melchizedek'"
>
> Heb 7:17

Melchizedek had no origin and no genealogy; He was a king, but also a priest of the most High God (Gen 14:18), and his life revealed the Christ to come.

As individuals we need to function in the dimensions of the key of David, but as a corporate church and body of the living God we need to move into, and function in, the order of Melchizedek, where the whole Body of Christ will express the dimensions of the priestly, prophetic and kingly role. It is good for the world to see individuals move and function in the way that God has called them to function in, but it is when the corporate body functions the way in which God has called it to function, that the world will start to pay close attention and will experience the Christ of whom we speak, serve and reveal to the broken and lost world!

There are certain paradigms that need to be changed in our thinking in order for this shift to take place. The church must:
- Break with all man-made tradition.
- Restore the order of things in the House of the Lord – God first.
- Move out of their comfort zones.
- Come back to the Word of God and leave doctrines of man (1 Tim 4:1&2; 1 Tim 6:3-5).
- Allow the Holy Spirit to move as He wills and follow His leading (John 14:16,17&26).
- Receive revelation of the purpose of the church and move according to the vision and mandate God has for that specific part of the body (church group). Do not do something because another church is also doing it.
- Receive revelation of the purpose of the five-fold ministry and allow these chosen ministers of God to function (Eph 4:11-16).
- Allow reformation in the individual's heart so that the revival will not stay in the

church but will go to the streets of the cities of the world! Revival was never meant to stay inside a building; it is to flow out (Acts 19).

It is time for the Church of God to stop all dead works, to stop talking, and to start living Christ. It is time to rise up, take responsibility, and be the voice in the wilderness that declares His love and rule to all creation, even the principalities of the air (Eph 3:10). The time has come for the different churches and denominations to rise in unity of spirit and deed to prepare the way of our King; for this is our destiny: To reveal the King of kings and Lord of lords.

You are born and destined to be the bride of Christ. Let us be prepared for that consummation of the ages where we will rule in all eternity with our Lord!

APPLICATION STUDY GUIDE FOR CHAPTER EIGHT

1. Do you fully understand the moving into the order of Melchizedek? Take time to allow the Holy Spirit to solidify these principles in your mind and spirit by:
   a. Reading the chapter or parts of the chapter that you are uncertain about again.
   b. Studying the following scripture:
      - Heb 8:7-13
2. What can you, as individual, do to help the body come to its destiny?
3. Pray for the Church of God to come into its destiny. Ask the Lord to shift the paradigms of church leaders and bless them:
   - To see what God has in store for them and their congregation.
   - To experience the Lord in a new level of relationship.
   - To apply the word of the Lord and His vision with wisdom.
   - Ask the Lord to give you scripture to declare over His body.

CHAPTER NINE

IN CONCLUSION

It is my heartfelt prayer that YOU will take what has been revealed in this book and make it part of your life. Allow the Lord to lead you and guide you as you learn each principle and then apply it in your life.

So much has been said, and sometimes the information may be overwhelming, but take just that which the Holy Spirit reveals to you and work it out until you live that principle without exerting effort. Then, move on to the next one. All that has been written in this book is as a result of revelations that the Lord has revealed to me over a period of three years. It has been an amazing learning curve and journey for me too, and one that I will never forget. The Lord has changed the way I think and see Him. I challenge you, now that you have come to the end of this book, to read it again, and you are bound to see things that have 'escaped' you, or you will just receive further revelation of what you already know.

Even now, when I teach on 'The Key of David', the Lord still reveals new things to me and He shows me areas in my life in which I need to apply these principles. We are never too young to start learning and certainly never too old to stop learning, especially when we learn from the Creator Himself.

I further trust that you will discover a whole new way of living as a beloved child of God and that you will enter into a deeper relationship with Him. Eph 3:20 says, "Now to Him who is able to do far more abundantly beyond all that we ask or think, according to the power that works within us."

I do not think that we can grasp the fullness of this one verse! God can do so much more than what we ask for or even think of. This means that there are things that have not even crossed our minds yet that He can do; the best part is that God does these things in ABUNDANCE! The wonder of it all is that His power works within our lives! What an awesome God we serve; we have the great privilege of calling Him 'Daddy'.

This is my prayer for you:
"May the Lord bless you and keep you; may His Face shine upon you and may He be gracious to you. May you experience His love for you like never before and may the Lord ignite a flame of passion in your heart this day that will never be quenched, no matter what happens. I declare that this flame will start rising in you from this moment and that you will not be able to get away from it.

You will be transformed by the Holy Spirit and you will find destiny beginning to unlock in your life. The Lord will cause destiny to search you out and find you and it will stir in you until you respond!

You will function in all the dimensions of 'The Key of David', and you will grow in them as you function in them.

May God's mercy and grace abound upon you as you do His will, and may He release boldness in you so that you may stand strong no matter what the circumstances are.

I bless you in the fullness of the name of Jesus Christ, out Lord and Saviour. Amen."

BIBLIOGRAPHY

Pulling Down Strongholds (DVD series)　　Dr. Jonathan David
Apostolic Strategies Affecting Nations　　Dr. Jonathan David
Apostolic Blueprints for Accurate Building　　Dr. Jonathan David

The Key of David (DVD teaching)　　Rev. Michael Pitts

Notes taken at the Apostolic Patterns
Retreat – Anchorage, Alaska; 2004　　Apostle Thamo Naidoo

For more information about the course "The Key of David" and other courses presented by Lion of Judah Ministries please contact:

Lion of Judah Ministries
PO Box 80236, Windhoek, Namibia.
E-mail: office@lionofjudahmin.com
Web: www.lionofjudahmin.com

www.ingramcontent.com/pod-product-compliance
Lightning Source LLC
Chambersburg PA
CBHW071309040426
42444CB00009B/1947